...the story is packed with surprises and emotional and spiritual rewards. The tale truly takes the reader on a spiritual journey. This work differs from other books about pilgrimages in that it is, in many respects, a love story, engagingly describing the author's quest to fulfill his dreams about learning, in as many senses as possible, the ways of the remarkable man who taught simple, truthful lessons and experienced a particularly deep connection to God.

-U.S Review of Books

Eanes masterfully weaves the story of St. Francis of Assisi into the story of his pilgrimage... Because of this inclusion of Francis' life, I felt as if I were right next to [him] walking with him and his wife, Jane.

—Dan Salerno, author of *20 Short Ones,* and *Metropolis: Tales From a Small Town*

Reading Pilgrim Paths to Assisi, the Way of Saint Francis comes alive ... skillfully interweaving stories from Saint Francis's life, musings on the meaning of pilgrimage, and practical advice for those hoping to undertake this 300-mile journey. Delightful descriptions of scenery, food, and people met along the way take readers into the heart of Apennines, and insightful reflections inspire contemplation about Saint Francis's relevance in a contemporary world.

—Matt Harms, Author of *The Way of St. Francis* and other pilgrimage guidebooks

PILGRIM PATHS TO ASSISI

300 Miles on the Way of St. Francis

RUSS EANES

The Walker Press

The Walker Press

www.thewalkerpress.com

ISBN softcover: 978-1-7333036-4-4

ISBN ebook: 978-1-7333036-5-1

Library of Congress Control Number: 2023908281

Cover photo by Jane Eanes. All other photos are by the author.

Cover design by Andre Eanes

Contact the author at russeanes.com

 Created with Vellum

To my children: Nate, Carolyn, Francis, Giles, Alli and Andre.
Being your Dad has been life's greatest journey.
Pax et Bonum

Also by Russ Eanes

The Walk of a Lifetime: 500 Miles on the Camino de Santiago

Contents

Italy

Florence

Assisi

Rome

The Way of St. Francis

Florence

La Verna

Gubbio

Assisi

Spoleto

Poggio Bustone

Rieti

Rome

N

100 km

60 mi

Author's Note

The journeys in this book are linear—I (we) start in one point and end in another. But those journeys are not always consecutive. I have walked the entire Way of St. Francis, just not in one go, though the destination has always been Assisi, the spiritual heart of Italy. To tell the story best—and to give you the best sense of what walking it is like—I begin the story in the middle of those three journeys, starting from Florence in the north, in April 2022. The second part starts at the other end, in Rome, in September 2022 and journeys north, but not all the way to Assisi. I stopped in Rieti, which is where the third part picks up, going back to our first journey in 2019. I hope this makes sense to the reader.

Introduction: Francis and His Ways

Everywhere the way of the pilgrim is twofold, the exterior and the interior, the simultaneous movement of the feet and the soul through time as well as space

Phil Cousineau, *The Art of Pilgrimage*

Francis brought the world a life of radical simplicity, unmoored to possessions and therefore free to follow the promptings of grace and the path toward God, wherever and whenever God summoned him. His spirit was one of remarkable spontaneity: he leaped to the needs of others, just as he hurried to catch up with God, who was always inviting him to a new adventure.

Donald Spoto, *Reluctant Saint: The Life of Francis of Assisi*

This is the story of a pilgrimage to Assisi on the Way of St. Francis—several pilgrimages actually: three on foot and one inward of the spirit. The journeys on foot took six weeks, over the course of several years; the inward one—to be inspired and even transformed by the life of Francis of Assisi —began decades ago and continues today, as all inner journeys should.

The outward journey to Assisi began in 2018 in Santiago de Compostela in northwestern Spain as I entered the crowded western plaza outside the legendary cathedral. I had just completed a 500-mile pilgrimage on foot. Walking the Camino de Santiago was the culmination of a dream that had bubbled along in my life for 20 years. In that journey I had joined my steps with the millions who had walked before me. It was a walk through space, time, and history.

That pilgrimage was life-changing, and I knew that I wanted to do something like this every year for as long as I lived. I had started that walk solo, but my wife, Jane, joined me during the last week. We entered the plaza together that day—a day I still regard as one of the most significant of my life. We decided that we would take another pilgrimage, this time in Italy along the Way of St. Francis, but first I needed to complete my book about walking the Camino de Santiago. Over decades, we had been moved by reading about the life of Francis, even naming our second son after him. We always planned one day visit Assisi, his birthplace and home.

Unlike the Camino de Santiago, the pilgrimage to Assisi would not take place over a matter of weeks but over a matter of years, with starts, stops, and the COVID-19 pandemic in the middle of it. While the pandemic and the focus on Francis made this pilgrimage different, it did not in any way diminish the journey's power, and in some ways it might have enhanced it.

≈

The Way of St. Francis (*Via di San Francesco* in Italian) is an atypical modern pilgrim path.[1] It starts in Florence in the north and ends in Rome in the south. It stretches 550 kilometers (340 miles). Several recent guidebooks more or less follow this route in part or in whole,[2] dividing it into 27 or 28 stages. On the map it has the shape of an arc, curving southeasterly through Tuscany and then Umbria, before straightening and bending more southwesterly through Lazio and toward Rome. It climbs and descends—repeatedly—the Apennine Mountains of central Italy. Traversing the mountains and foothills is challenging, and the distances belie the fact that there is a lot of climbing. From Florence to Rome, the path has an elevation gain of about 16,000 meters.[3]

Unlike the Camino de Santiago, this route for pilgrims has only been created in recent decades, but many of the pathways it follows are ancient, tramped for centuries, even millennia. Its essence is its linking of dozens of significant places in the life of Francis, places of legend, places of refuge and retreat, places where he may have performed a miracle or preached, and places where he slept or had divine revelations.

The path enchants pilgrims with all the sensual delights of central Italy as it passes mile after mile of olive groves and vineyards, climbs rocky mountain paths, reveals spectacular vistas over wide river valleys, and winds through ancient stone villages and monasteries. It fords streams and crosses rivers, cuts deep into ancient forests where the only sound is the cuckoo. It exudes its own mystical aura, not unlike the deep, mystical spirit of Francis himself. It skirts, and occasionally enters, hilltop towns and cities, some of which appear to be cut from rocky promontories. It passes medieval castles, some still fortified with defensive walls and towers, reminiscent of Italy's volatile political past. It is rocky, it is paved; it is dirt, it is gravel. It is wild beauty and richly cultivated simplicity. The mountain passes smell of thyme, rosemary, and oregano; the villages of wisteria. It requires vigorous climbs and occasional treacherous, rocky descents. It winds through history, through culture, through fabulous local cuisines. It is ancient stone churches with peeling frescoes, it is abandoned villas and overgrown orchards. It is physically and mentally challenging. It is silent, it is lush, it is remote, it is hospitable.

Some of the most significant places include "sanctuaries" and hermitages, places where Francis and his early followers could retreat from the crowds and find solitude, similar to what Jesus and his disciples did. It includes small chapels where he frequently prayed and magnificent basilicas, places that today may contain a letter written in his hand or an item of his clothing. His most isolated hermitages are as dramatic as they are beautiful: often at significant heights, up the sides of mountains, out on a precipice, down into a deep rock cleft, or inside a cave. The most famous of these are routinely visited by tour busses, but some of the most striking and mysterious (and my favorite) are accessible only on foot.

Linked along the Way are cities and towns, such as charming Gubbio, with its steep, narrow streets and medieval quarter, where Francis supposedly tamed a wolf that terrorized the locals, or Greccio, where he staged the first live Christmas reenactment, animals and all. Others are places of miracles, such as La Foresta, where he produced a miraculous crop of grapes, or La Verna, where he reportedly received the stigmata (the wounds of Christ) on his body. Some are more mundane, like Foligno, where he sold his father's cloth for cash to give to the poor.

The ascents and occasional remote stretches between these places can seem daunting. The best approach is to walk them in smaller segments, keeping in mind the elevation gains as much as the distances. The climbs force you to slow down and take in the surroundings, to expect and experience a bit more mystery.

Weaving together the legends and history of Francis along the ancient paths make this a unique pilgrimage; at times you can still sense his presence there. Moreover, it is versatile; you can start and end anywhere along its route.

Assisi, Francis's hometown in central Umbria, is the halfway point. It stands above the rest, both literally and figuratively. Sitting like a jewel on an outcrop of Mount Subasio, it is the place where he was born and died, the departure point for a life of purposeful wandering, preaching, and ministry. In its basilica, his mortal remains are preserved and have been venerated for over 800 years. I chose Assisi as the final destination for each of my three journeys along the route, for I consider it to be the heart of this pilgrimage.

He offered his followers, quite simply, a better life, a more joyful life, one that provided the kind of satisfaction that comes to a commitment to something other than money. They found him and his message irresistible
Donald Spoto, *Reluctant Saint: The Life of Francis of Assisi*

Giovanni Bernadone, known to us in history as Saint Francis (*San Francesco* in Italian), was born in Assisi in 1181 or 1182. He died there 44 years later, a short life by modern standards but outsized in its impact on his own time and on history. He lived more in those four decades than many live in a life twice as long.

Francis—alongside Jesus, Moses, Mohammed, and Buddha—is one of the world's most widely known, beloved, and revered religious figures. According to contemporary Franciscan speaker and author Richard Rohr, "When Pope John Paul II wanted to gather the leaders of all the world religions to have a respectful interfaith dialogue in the 1980s, the only city in the world that they could agree to meet in was Assisi, because the memory of St. Francis does not carry any negative baggage, even to other religions."[4] Books about his life and references about him in books proliferate. Apparently, he has the longest card catalog entry of any person in the Library of Congress.[5] In Italian he's *Il Poverello*, "The Little Poor Man," and he's the patron saint of Italy, along with Catherine of Siena. Since 1986 he is the patron saint of the worldwide ecological movement. In an age of disbelief, skepticism, evangelical fervor, and religious extremism, his wide acceptance comes as a welcome relief. In an age of overconsumption that is heating an already ecologically threatened planet, his life of simplicity and care for the natural world points to hope. The current Pope—eager to emphasize his own commitment to the poor of the world—even became history's first Pope Francis.

Francis's father, Pietro Bernadone, was a wealthy cloth merchant among the emerging middle classes of Umbria in central Italy. His mother, Pica, was possibly French, or at least knew French, and called her son Francesco (Francis in English), meaning "little Frenchy," and the nickname stuck. Pietro took his son on journeys to France and Belgium where he traded for the latest in fabrics. Along the way the young Francesco would have learned the medieval, romantic tales and songs of the troubadours, legends of courtly love and valiant knights. They remained with him during his life, the poetry and music influencing his preaching. His own poem, *Canticle of the Sun,* is credited as being the first poem written in Italian (versus Latin).[6]

Francesco received an education and enjoyed the privileges associated with being the son of wealth. He caroused with the sons of other affluent merchants and nobility, sponsoring drinking parties and earning a reputation as a bit of a playboy. Like many other young men of his age, he longed for the glories of warfare. To win his reputation he went with several of his fellows to battle with neighboring Perugia, outfitted in an expensive suit of armor. But he was to win neither riches nor glory; he was captured during the brief battle, which ended in a humiliating defeat for Assisi. He suffered for two years in a damp and cold prison, while peace was negotiated and ransom was raised for his release.

Accounts of what happened next vary and even conflict, but this much is agreed upon: He returned home a changed man. This was the beginning of an ongoing and gradual conversion leading to a dramatic and painful confrontation with his own father, when he stripped himself—figuratively and literally—of his family's wealth and station and embraced a life of voluntary poverty. He spent the next two decades wandering, preaching, and caring for the poor and sick, especially lepers. He poured out this love to those he met, impressing those who heard his simple sermons and having a profound effect wherever he went. The common person, feeling distant from God through the practices of the Roman Catholic Church, now felt God very near and approachable. In a time of near-continuous warfare and political and religious foment, Francis stood out as a Christlike figure. Like Christ he invited people to follow, and follow they did, in the tens of thousands. Among the throngs who came to follow him were the "cream" of Assisi's youth, the offspring of other wealthy Italians who also chose the path of voluntary poverty. This included Clare, a young woman who created a scandal similar to Francis's when she chose to follow his life of service to the poor. He called his followers "friars minor" or "little brothers," a term taken from the social orders of the time, in which the *minore* were at the bottom of society, just above the outcasts.

~

> Throughout his life from now on Francis emanated an almost radioactive energy which seemed to derive from his continuous proximity to God. It was said he didn't love God, but was in love with him. To live in his company was therefore formidable yet also exhilarating, for his conviction was infectious and communicated to many of his companions a faith as luminescent as his. United in everything they did, they quickly discovered a degree of trust, purpose and collective happiness they had never remotely experienced before.
>
> Adrian House, *Francis of Assisi: A Revolutionary Life*

His welcoming spirit and love of animals—indeed the entire natural world—appealed to those who felt that God (and the church) were too otherworldly and removed from the everyday experience of the common person. Popes, kings, the nobility and the wealthy, scholars and clerics also were drawn to him. He inspired them to leave everything and follow him—some during his lifetime, many in the generations after his death. He preached peace, at risk to his life, to both Christians and Muslims in Egypt during the Third Crusade. The Sultan was so impressed by Francis that he honored him with a hearing and treated him with deep respect.[7]

Assisi initially rejected Francis but eventually came to revere him. Francis died there in 1226 and was made a saint in 1228, perhaps the fastest canonization in history. This movement had, paradoxically, received the approval of the powerful Roman Catholic Church, though at its very core it represented values that directly contradicted the institution. The Roman Catholic Church raised a magnificent basilica to house his remains, completed in two years, a record time for such church construction in the Late Middle Ages. More significant than the basilica is the lasting spiritual impact Francis has had on Christianity and other religions and faith traditions.

> Francis does not really provide many systematic answers to theological questions as much as he *is* a living answer to those who ask the right questions.
>
> Richard Rohr, *Eager to Love: The Alternative Way of Francis of Assisi*

My own fascination with Francis began with the film *Brother Sun, Sister Moon*, which I saw in my early twenties, while in seminary. The film is visually lush, its message striking.

I was struck by Francis's deep spirituality, commitment to God, and dedication to his calling.

I was struck by his simplicity and delight in the natural world.

I was struck by his nonjudgmental, gracious spirit and his nonviolence.

I was struck by his deep humanity and love for all living things (including animals), but the poor in particular.

I was struck by his willingness to give up security, privilege, and material comforts.

I was struck by the freedom that he gained, by giving up society's most cherished securities, including status. I was reminded of the words of Jesus, who said that to "gain" our life, we must "lose" it.[8]

These things constitute the "inner way" of Francis, a way that has impacted millions over the centuries.

I left seminary before completing a divinity degree, as my own sense of vocation and calling took a different turn. But I never stopped learning about Francis or feeling impacted by him. Over the next decades I read several biographies of his life, while my wife and growing family and I embraced a life of service and material simplicity, all in pursuit of many of the same spiritual longings and ideals of Francis. The peace we sought was a response to the same anxieties, conflicts, stresses, and never-ending preoccupations with money, possessions, and social status that Francis renounced and that are possibly even greater and more oppressive in our time.

We joined first one, then a second, intentional Christian community—something like a commune—beginning in a poor, urban area, then later in a rural context, closer to nature and the outdoors. We lived there 14 years while our children grew, then in 1998 decided that we would "reenter" society in order to be closer to my aging parents. This meant earning our own living and re-acquiring personal possessions, but we kept our lifestyle simple. We made sure, as much as possible, to stay focused on the values that Francis stood for—his message of peace, of service, of love and grace for others, care for the poor and for the natural world.

~

At about the same time our family made that transition 25 years ago, my own spiritual understanding and outlook expanded. I became fascinated with the spiritual aspects of pilgrimage. I felt drawn to make a pilgrimage on foot to some of the most famous sites, starting in Europe. I hungered to visit places of significant spiritual history, places where the past still lives, "thin places" where the spiritual and mystical break through the physical. I traveled to some, such as Iona and Lindisfarne in the United Kingdom, Newgrange and Glendalough in Ireland, and Vézelay in France. I stood in awe before Canterbury Cathedral and dozens of other medieval cathedrals in France, Switzerland, and Germany, finally culminating in 2018 when I made my long-awaited pilgrimage to Santiago. My hope was that pilgrimage on foot would become an ongoing part of our lives for as long as we could still strap on a backpack and move our feet.

My Franciscan impulses reawakened and I felt drawn next to Umbria and to Assisi. I wanted to see the land of Francis, to take in its scents, feel its stones, touch its soil. I wanted to experience the remoteness, the solitude, the quiet of the mountains and the paths that challenged and fed the mind, spirit, and soul of Francis. I wanted to feel inwardly the places of his history. So, after we returned home, we began to prepare for our next pilgrimage, one that would complete the circle of faith, discovery, and spiritual longing to understand and appreciate Francis that had begun four decades earlier. This book is that story.

~

In 2018 as I prepared to walk to Santiago de Compostela, I developed a set of seven principles that guided me on my journey, and they served me well. On subsequent pilgrimages, I expanded and modified that list, and it is now up to twelve. I share these "Pilgrimage Principles" at the outset of this book as they provide a framework to the meaningful journey that I am about to share with you.

While these principles are woven into my time spent along the Way of St. Francis, they also are helpful for all of life.

1. Keep your pack light.
2. Don't be in a hurry.
3. Absorb your surroundings with all your senses.
4. Accept whatever is offered you, as a gift from God.
5. Walk in expectation of the unexpected.
6. Keep plans flexible and adapt as you go.
7. Accept your limitations.
8. Greet and take interest in other pilgrims; offer them something if they need it.
9. Have reverence for those who have walked before you.
10. Appreciate the locals and get to know them. Sample their foods.
11. Read historical markers. Touch the stones.
12. Leave behind somewhere an appropriate token.

PART I

Florence to Assisi, April 2022

290 kilometers
10,100 meters elevation

An Arduous Journey

When the scales of laziness fall over our eyes and we have begun to take life for granted, we must take an arduous journey to relearn the essential truths of the life right before our eyes.

Phil Cousineau, *The Art of Pilgrimage*

ONE MIGHT NOT IMAGINE that an arduous journey could begin in Florence, birthplace of the Renaissance, a *Patrimonio Mondiale,* a UNESCO World Heritage Site. Cultured Florence, which gave us Dante, Machiavelli, the Medici, and Michelangelo and which today is known as Europe's art capital, is itself a work of art. With its stately *piazzas,* richly decorated churches, iconic Duomo, bustling, narrow streets, high-end boutiques, crowded restaurants, sidewalk cafés, colorful flowers, well-appointed gardens, and famed Ponte Vecchio—Florence is the essence of the Italian *Dolce Vita,* the "sweet life," celebrating beauty, comfort, and ease.

Despite that, amid the splendid weather in mid-April, as the city exerted its seductive pull and tourists streamed in, my wife and I headed out to begin our arduous journey.[1] People could be excused for thinking we were crazy, leaving one of the world's most historic and beautiful cities less than 24 hours after we had arrived. Our destination was Assisi, 290 kilometers and 17 days away. We were continuing a journey we had begun more than two years earlier that had been stalled by the COVID-19 pandemic, heading out to find the places of St. Francis somewhere in the mountains to the east and south. On the previous journey we had approached Assisi from the south, starting in Rieti, but now, following the convention of the guidebooks, we were coming at it from the other direction.

Walking to the mountains—and through them—was going to be the arduous part. Heading that way, we were reversing history, leaving the chic present and heading backward through the Second World War, Mussolini, and Fascism; backward through the *Risorgimento*, or unification of Italy in the 19th century; backward through the Renaissance, the birth of the Italian city-state and communes; backward to the age of Francis in the early 13th century; and backward even beyond that, nearly 3,000 years, to the Roman Empire and to the Etruscans.

～

FLORENCE, founded as a colony for former soldiers in 59 B.C.E. by the Romans at a ford in the Arno River, was still struggling to become a Republic in the late 12th century when Francis was born. Its treasured Duomo and Ponte Vecchio had yet to be built, its first gold *florin*, a standard of medieval coinage, had yet to be minted. As an up-and-coming power center, Florence, not unlike Rome, figured small in the life of Francis. But our guidebook started the journey there, so there we began the part of the Way of St. Francis that would be for us the most arduous, and likewise the most rewarding.

Ahead there were mountains to climb and the deep and remote Casentino Forest. I had read that the isolated pathways could be rocky, muddy, even slippery; the route markers might be confusing and at times nonexistent. We would have to rely on our phones for navigation. As grueling as the steep climbs could be, going down would be even slower and more treacherous. The high mountain passes are long, lonely, windy, and potentially chilly in spring.

The small towns are farther apart from one another. Occasionally we would have to haul extra water and packed lunches. On top of it all, we hardly knew the language. We would have to rely on our basic Italian vocabulary, smiles, and bits of Spanish.

All this I knew. But there were other challenges ahead that would make the journey even more arduous than we anticipated.

Lodging wasn't always available. We were booking our rooms only one or two days ahead as part of our Pilgrimage Principle 6, to "keep plans flexible and adapt." Sometimes the hoped-for host didn't answer the phone or email. We were starting to walk during Holy Week and were competing with weekend hikers, vacationers, and pilgrim-tourists in cars or buses who sometimes took all available rooms in B&Bs, *rifugios* (mountain inns), and hotels. The Way is not solely oriented toward walking pilgrims.

Occasionally the bed was too hard, the room too hot or too cold. Some hosts did not speak or understand a word of English and didn't grasp that we didn't understand a single thing they were saying; one of them was in her eighties and hard of hearing.

Some churches I had hoped to visit—sacred places in which to pause and reflect—were closed. A few times, heavy clouds rumbled in from the horizon and the downpour turned the path into a river. Just as suddenly the cloudburst was over, we had to stop to peel off our raincoats, and before long we sweltered in the sun.

And then there was the path itself. Streams that our guidebook said could be easily crossed on dry stones had swelled with spring rains, leaving no dry crossing. Ahead or behind spring storms, stiff winds buffeted us on the high passes and trees fell over the path. We had to duck underneath, scramble around, or climb over them. Our legs grew tired, and yet the map showed another climb ahead. Progress was sometimes slow.

I had my own insecurities: Could I haul my now-65-year-old body up the steep ascents of the Apennines? What about my knees on the long descents? What would it feel like to plunge into the deep and remote forests of the Casentino, miles from nowhere, the countryside and the mountains unknown to us? The pandemic, waning, was still on the periphery: How might/could it affect anything?

Jane had her own uncertainties. Along with me she'd studied the stages of the journey ahead, and the difficult climbing made her apprehensive. I knew that she was fit, loved to walk, and enjoyed these types of adventures once she was on them. But of the two of us, I was more of the adventurer, even known to be a bit reckless. Yet here she was joining me, in spite of any qualms about the journey ahead. I admired her willingness to face the challenge. How many other grandmothers, having earned a well-deserved retirement, would instead choose a 290-kilometer trek through steep, unknown mountains with a 7-kilo pack on their back?

"I may walk a bit slower than you. Will I be holding you back?" she had asked me as we made our plans. "No," I said, "the speed of the journey doesn't matter. Having you along to share it with me is more important than how fast we go. And I'm so glad you know Spanish; you'll probably be a lot better than me at communicating in Italian." That was no small thing: I was delighted for her to be in charge of figuring out the lodging and communicating with hosts, a tedious task for me and one that she enjoyed.

If we had let them, the fears could have defined the journey. Yet what we sensed before we left and learned with certainty along the way was that it was the unknown, the thrill of the challenges, that make life—and pilgrimage—all the more rewarding. We discovered that by plunging into it with a bit of abandon, with faith, by laying aside our fears and opening ourselves to the unexpected provisions that a pilgrimage offers, wonderful things transpired and they, not our fears, defined the journey. The unknowns could even be said to make it more "authentically Franciscan" as we relied on others, on serendipity, on chance. Francis himself had endured the same challenges as he traversed these very hills, relying on the generosity and goodwill of others.

Lodging full? A host with good English and a cheery voice calls back about a nicer accommodation and offers to pick us up, then provides us a four-course, homemade Tuscan meal.

Feet tired? An unplanned shortcut slices an hour and a few miles off the route, or a bus stop appears along the highway with a bus arriving in minutes to ferry us along when we can't go a step further.

Hot? The long deep silence in the cool of the forest

becomes a welcome companion after an hour in the beating sun.

Fatigued? We arrive hungry and weary, and our hosts unexpectedly place a delicious meal—and a tall beer—in front of us.

Wet? The rain stops, the sun comes out, and wet clothes quickly dry. The clouds break open or the mists lift, unveiling a stunning vista over the mountains.

Hungry? The path down from the mountain pass is smooth with a village around a bend where a sandwich, a pastry, and a cappuccino lift our mood.

Can't cross the stream? A pilgrim-angel appears from nowhere and points to a shallow crossing that we haven't seen.

Trees blocking the path? A man with a chainsaw is there to cut them away.

Out of water? More pilgrim-angels materialize and give two liters to us.

Simplicity reigns: A picnic lunch, some buns purchased in the bread shop, and some cheese and fruit from the small *alimentari* (local food markets) are spread out on a grassy meadow. Together with the mountain vista they become a banquet.

Fellow pilgrims, seekers, and wanderers, bring conversation and exchange snacks, smiles, and encouragement. We become one with them and then part ways just as easily.

The door to an 11th-century church is surprisingly open, and inside is a beautifully preserved slice of medieval architecture and modest piety, complete with ancient frescoes. Its peace enters your heart as you sit in silence.

For all our apprehensions, we found comfortable beds, delicious meals, warm hosts, hot and soothing showers. We discovered that with our tiny bit of Italian and Spanish and our hosts' smattering of English, we could even pass an entire evening making deep connections.

Busy streets of Florence

THE JOURNEY BEGAN as we shouldered our packs (about 7 kilos or 15 pounds each) and stepped onto the narrow sidewalk along the jostling, chaotic street outside our Florence hotel. Horns honked. A steady wind blew down the urban canyonland of five-story stone buildings. Pedestrians flowed in both directions, dodging the scooters and bicycles that zipped by: adults on their way to work, kids on their way to school, tourists heading for the museums. The warm air stank slightly of diesel. Workers shouted to each other from atop scaffolding as we ducked beneath it. An occasional car inched its way through the throng.

It was going to be a perfect day for walking. Though we hadn't completely recovered from jet lag, we had energy and excitement, and a spring in our step.

We had to be careful navigating out of the city. In Florence the streets twist, turn, and can suddenly end, and the names can change. Our route seemed straightforward, though in the city there were no markers or signposts showing us the way. Until we hit the countryside there would be no blazes on trees, no signs to mark the route. I had a guidebook with a map but chose to navigate with my iPhone, the most modern of pilgrim devices, which would always pinpoint our location and make sure we stayed on the correct path.

Heading northeast from our hotel near the central train station, we passed the Via dell'Ariento, home of the Mercato Centrale, a street lined with booth after booth of leather jackets and purses. Florence is known for its leather goods, and the hawkers, holding up an item, relentlessly called "*Trenta euro!*" to us. But we ignored them. I wasn't shopping, and the last thing I wanted was more weight in my pack.

Typically, pilgrims start their journey in front of the Basilica di Santa Croce, the world's largest Franciscan church and the place where the first *timbro* or stamp on the *credenziale* (pilgrim passport) might be obtained. We had gone there the day before to get ours stamped, but since we were staying on the other side of the city, we had decided that our journey would begin at the hotel. A shorter and more level route of about 19 kilometers heads directly east along the Arno toward Pontassieve, the end of the first day's stage. We chose instead to follow an older route that would take us up into the surrounding foothills, where we could get a glimpse of Florence's skyline. It was about 4 kilometers longer, 23 kilometers in all, and would require more climbing before the descent back to Compiobbi where we would rejoin the more level route along the Arno about nine kilometers from Pontassieve.

Walking through the city, we passed the crowds queuing up to enter the Accademia, one of the most famous of Florence's art galleries, and home to Michelangelo's most famous sculpture, *David*. We continued past the delightful botanical garden, the Giardino dei Semplici, and before long entered the wide and green Piazza della Libertà. We went through the tall Porta San Gallo and stood in front of the triumphal arch across from it.[2]

Porta San Gallo

FROM HERE ON, I had to consult the route via my phone more frequently. We went under a railroad track. We wound clockwise at roundabouts and twisted and turned with the route. The road and the sky became gradually wider after leaving the Piazza della Libertà, the scenery more suburban. The hills grew nearer, with their green parklands. We crossed another intersection, the road narrowed, and the sidewalk disappeared. Cars still whizzed by too closely, but within minutes the traffic thinned, and after a few more turns and bends we were finally away from the cars, to our relief.

The columnar cypress along the road

Our route gradually led us upward into the foothills. The air freshened as the traffic disappeared and the sky widened into a classically Tuscan panorama of stone villas, columnar cypresses, and the distinctive *Pinus pinea* (umbrella pine). This Mediterranean native can grow up to 25 meters or 80 feet in height. It was a typical feature in the landscape of ancient Rome. Rosemary bloomed everywhere, its lavender flowers cascading over stone walls, splashing the hillsides with color along with the white apple blossoms and cherry trees decked in pink. Instead of noisy traffic, there was the loud buzz of bees flying from blossom to blossom. Instead of diesel fumes, there was the fragrance of the wisteria draped over gateways.

We hardly thought about the weight on our backs. We felt at home on the trail, and our spirits remained light with each step. I had been worried about some pain in my knees during the weeks before we left, but out here my sense of wonder grew and any doubts about myself vanished. Any worry about my knees disappeared.

A grassy path along a blooming apple orchard lifted us above the road and past a small settlement toward a tall, castle-like tower. It was the charming Castello di Mezzaratta, which, though looking medieval, was just a century old. We passed it and after a brief climb arrived at the Piazza Desiderio, where we turned to see the magnificent vista over the city.

Looking south, we saw the distinctive orange Duomo and its smaller twin dome, San Lorenzo. Farther east we could see the twin towers in the Piazza della Signoria and the long, distinctive profile of Santa Croce. Farther east, the Apennines grew considerably higher and closer.

We continued east a short distance into the village of Sentignano, and since it was noon and we had been walking for three hours, we bought some cold, bottled water in a café, then stepped into the central plaza, pulled off our packs, and sat down in some shade. The ice-cold water was refreshing and the break rejuvenating, but we wanted to press onward, so we soon shouldered our packs and continued our journey.

For another hour we continued along a quiet road that was alternately dirt and paved. We passed luxurious villas with small vineyards, olive groves with their ancient, gnarled trunks dotted the hillsides. All around we saw tall and brilliant redbud trees. I had been missing our own redbud in bloom at home but discovered that the Mediterranean had its own, the *Cercis siliquastrum* (Judas tree), a variety native to southern Europe. We finally saw our first route markers: the red and white blazes of the *Club Alpina Italiano* (Italian Hiking Club or CAI). Much of the Way of St. Francis follows the club's hiking routes. We also came upon the blue and yellow blazes of the Way of St. Francis itself and the five-sided "official" route markers of the Via di Francesco Toscana.

IT WAS midafternoon when we descended to Compiobbi, where we joined the shorter and flatter route from Florence. It was a good time to stop and have lunch, so we made our way into the town. We picked up some sandwiches in a café and asked them to refill our water bottles, then found a place along the river to have our picnic and watch the Arno flow by lazily. We could hear the distant sounds of trucks on the highway across the river, but it was an otherwise peaceful spot. Ducks floated down the river past a few old men fishing. I leaned back on my pack and momentarily closed my eyes.

I could have taken a nap, but it was now after 2:30 and I thought it might be better to find the bed in our B&B in

Pontassieve. That bed was still nine kilometers ahead, close to two hours of walking. With determination we got to our feet and headed upriver, then cut inland, crossed the railroad tracks, and in another three kilometers arrived back at the river in the town of Le Sieci. The dirt trail along the river was peaceful, and it was tempting to stop again, but we could see Pontassieve just a few kilometers ahead. We passed through the town, crossed a small highway, and went under the train tracks, which followed the river all the way from Florence

I looked at my guidebook and my GPX tracks.[3] The book and GPX pointed back up into the foothills, but it was clear that an alternate path ran alongside the railroad directly into Pontassieve. It turned out to be way-marked for the Via Francesco. Going directly would be shorter, involve less climbing, and get us to that B&B and a nap sooner. We could see locals walking this path with their dogs. We chose to go more directly.

A quiet path through Le Sieci

With the determination that comes from the first day of a long pilgrimage, we walked on in silence, our minds too tired for conversation. On our right, over a fence, was the railway; on our left were empty plowed fields below the foothills we had gladly chosen not to climb, despite their vistas. The eagerness for our final destination and a bed and shower propelled us forward in spite of our physical and mental fatigue.

The path soon dove into a small wood, and within five

minutes we were on the edge of Pontassieve, cars once again whizzing by us as we entered town and found our B&B. It was now after 5:00. The owners, friendly but knowing no English, showed us our room, where we showered, hand-washed clothes, and hung them up to dry before we finally caught a well-deserved nap. We arrived tired but agreed that everything about today's walk felt perfect, with the energy of two-and-a-half years of waiting relieved.

The journey ahead may be arduous, but we were on pilgrimage again, just where we wanted to be.

Pontassieve

The Medieval gate in Pontassieve.

2

Into the Mountains

The hills which only twenty-four hours before seemed noble and benevolent are now mountains, intimidating and unforgiving, looming rather than rolling, multiplying in size and number.

Simon Armitage, *Walking Home: A Poet's Journey*

PONTASSIEVE, on the western edge of the Apennines, is an ancient town, valued in the Middle Ages because of its bridge over the river Sieve, which slices through the mountains from the north, joining the Arno as it comes up from the south.[1] The bridge was built by the Medici. Ahead on our route, to the east, lay the vast Casentino Forest National Park, with its woodlands and upland river valleys. It has been a source of wool and timber for nearly a millennium, though both sheep and people have dwindled in number.

It was an important rail junction during the Second World War, so the town was unfortunately leveled by Allied bombers. A new, modern town arose from the rubble of the old, still surrounded on all sides by mountains and foothills with their patchwork of olive groves.

After our first day of walking, Jane and I had needed—and had gotten—a good night's rest and a good breakfast, and now our legs and spirits were refreshed. Since we didn't know where we might stop for lunch, we packed our things and headed to the enormous COOP *supermercato* to pick up sandwiches and fruit for the day.

With our food stashed in our backpacks, we followed the route to the other end of town and stopped to take pictures on the famed, ancient stone bridge over the Sieve. As I set down my trekking poles, I glanced at Jane, who realized at the same moment that she didn't have hers. Where could they be? She scanned her memory and blurted, "I left them at the COOP."

This wasn't the first lost or misplaced item during this journey, nor would it be the last. We backtracked to the store and, to our relief, found the poles standing upright where Jane had left them. Saint Anthony[2] must have been looking out for us, just as he must have been the day before when we misplaced (but later found) our room key in Florence, much to the relief of the hotel owner. We retraced our steps to the bridge, which we finally crossed, but we had lost half an hour.

This is where the guidebook says that the climb "begins in earnest." Indeed. While the paved Via del Tirolo starts as a shady and quiet country lane, it is steep. Our destination that day was the Passo della Consuma, the mountain pass along this ancient route into the Casentino. This was one of the most difficult stages: climbing 1,200 meters over 17 kilometers overall, almost a 7% grade. To give you a sense for this, some treadmills max out at a 10% incline, so this would be a steep uphill climb, on rocky soil, for more than 10 kilometers. This was the challenge that I had thought about the most when we had trained during climbs in the Blue Ridge Mountains near our home.

As we ascended, the scenery was gorgeous, even with the leaves not yet out on the trees. After climbing a few kilometers, we found ourselves under an inviting blue sky with wisps of white clouds. Wide vistas of vineyards and olive groves stretched to the mountains. An occasional hill was topped with a small castle or villa. One of those, an unmistakable landmark visible from the start, was the 11th-century Castello Nipozzano, crowning a nearby hilltop and overseeing the vast holdings of the Frescobaldi family, who have cultivated wine and olives in this region for 800 years. Their vineyards, which include grapes of Tuscany's most famous vintage, Chianti, stretched out in row after row of clean, trimmed, and staked but barren vines, waiting for the spring rains and a warm summer that would leave them heavily laden with bunches of grapes by September. The long rows with their neatly spaced poles and trellises created an undulating, geometric symmetry as it followed the contours of the hills.

The viniculture was older than even the Frescobaldi family; it was the Romans who had first developed this method of staking and training the vines. This region had been settled by the Romans and before that the Etruscans, a history going back over 3,000 years. (The name *Tuscany* comes from the word *Etruscan*.) This ancient, cultivated landscape of castles, vineyards, and olive groves is a defining feature of the Way of St. Francis as it snakes in and out of the wooded and wilder mountain passes on its way to Rome. Still to come were the monasteries, villages, and hilltop towns, all of which make this a unique pathway: We never knew where or when in history a climb would take us.

What made for a gorgeous vista also made for a hot sun, which by now was beating down on us and, along with the climb, was making us quite toasty. We guzzled water, shed several clothing layers, and began to calculate the distance to our next stop. After an hour the steep grade relaxed, fortunately, but under the wide blue sky, the sun now felt relentless.

Approaching Diacceto

WE LEFT the asphalt for a gravel road between the vineyards that gave way to a grassy track. After a few more kilometers we saw and heard the village of Diacceto, its church bell ringing the noon hour. We rejoined a shoulderless blacktop road just below the village, and the traffic passed uncomfortably close for the next five minutes until we were in the village. I spied a café and we crossed the road to reach it. This was our first stop—in two hours, we had climbed over 300 meters.

With my simple Italian, we managed to order tea for Jane and a cappuccino and pastries for me, and pulled out our sandwiches. The man behind the counter kindly refilled our water bottles as he conversed with a few locals standing at the counter.

Jane looked at me as she slowly ate her lunch. I knew what was on her mind: The jet lag we thought we'd shrugged off was creeping up on her, compounded by the climb, the heat, the sun, and the workout we'd had the day before; it was all proving to be too much. It was only early afternoon, and I knew she still had a bit of energy left, but the hardest part of the day's stage was yet to come.

"How much more climbing is there?" she asked.

"Let's see. The good news is we've already climbed about 300-plus meters. The total for today is close to 1,200. So, well, we haven't quite done a third of it yet." I paused, then added, "It's another 11 kilometers and 900 meters." I wanted to sound upbeat, but there was no way to sugarcoat what was still ahead.

Her face registered her dismay. "I'm sorry, but I just don't think I can do it," she said simply, with a mixture of frustration and disappointment. "I hate to give up in the middle of our second day, and I'd rather you didn't have to walk alone the rest of the way, but I'm just out of energy."

I need to explain something about Jane: my wife is tough and does not give up easily on anything. She relishes a challenge. Maybe, as the oldest of four, she was born that way. Maybe it was life's circumstances: she lost her father at age

17. Not to be daunted, she put herself through college entirely on her own, earning nearly straight A's. After we married, she raised six children, a feat made all the more challenging by our unconventional lifestyle choices. She's anything but a quitter. So if she was throwing in the towel it was because the combination of factors had proven truly overwhelming.

We knew that Diacceto, where we were, had no overnight options. Consuma, our destination, was the closest town with guest accommodations. I suggested, "It's time to come up with a plan 'b' for 'bus.'" This was something we had agreed on ahead of time. We just hadn't expected to have to resort to it so soon, but the next section of the hike was a part I wanted to experience. "Is it okay with you if I go on?" I asked. She nodded with equal parts of disappointment and relief.

Luckily, I had noticed a bus stop as we were walking into town. Consuma might be another 11 kilometers and at least three hours of walking, but it was only a 20-minute ride via the highway. I approached the man behind the counter and asked, in something between basic Italian and sign language, if that bus came today. He glanced down at his wristwatch. *"Sì, tredici e diece."* Thirteen ten. 1:10 p.m.

I looked at my watch. It was only 12:30, so we had plenty of time. I asked again in mixed Italian and English if he was *certain* it would be today. I pointed down to emphasize *today*. *"Oggi?"*

"Sì." But where to get a ticket? I knew that the *tabacchi*[3] was usually a place to get one. *"E biglietto?"*

He shook his head, *"Solo Internet."* Tickets for this route are purchased only online. *Rats,* I thought to myself, but in English.

Then he smiled, shook his head again, and waved his

hand dismissively to indicate that it didn't matter, the driver would not check. Relieved, we finished our lunch, paid for our food and drinks,[4] thanked him, and headed out the door and across the street to the bus stop.

I lingered with Jane awhile. Her face displayed a mixture of relief and mild disappointment: relief that she wouldn't have to do the tough climb ahead but disappointment that she would leave me to tackle it alone. "Am I just being a wimp?" she blurted out. "Not at all," I said reassuringly, reminding her that we had agreed as we were preparing for the walk that the bus would be an option on a tough day, and this was already one of those tough days. As I noted earlier, Jane is not one to give up easily, but taking the bus in this instance was not a failure but, rather, *wisdom*. We had done something similar in 2019 while walking the southern portion of the route, when on the second day we both already needed to take a bus for part of it. Pilgrimage gets easier as your body gets used to the long days of walking, so it can take your body a few days to adjust. It's a marathon, not a sprint. There is nothing sacred about walking every step of the path. More important is the overall journey, the pilgrimage, doing what is manageable and enjoying it as much as possible, *together*. Whenever I have spoken or written about our journey, I emphasize this point: The route is hard, and there are days when the best decision for either or both of us might be to cut it short or to take a bus or a taxi. It is Pilgrimage Principle 7, "Know your limitations."

I gave Jane a hug. I was slightly disappointed that she couldn't go with me, but I was even more glad and relieved that she had chosen her own pace, her own comfort level with this. I had a sense that it was a *very* difficult climb ahead. There would, in fact, be plenty more climbs to come, and she would eventually prove herself quite resilient. But for now, it was the bus, and that was best.

∼

> **APENNINES:** *AP eh nynz,* is the name of a mountain range which runs from the Gulf of Genoa to the toe of boot-shaped Italy. The range has three divisions, the Northern, the Central and the Southern Apennines. They cover about two thirds of the area of the Italian peninsula. These old mountains are among the lowest in Europe. They have been worn down by wind and rain for millions of years.
>
> *World Book Encyclopedia,* 1960

I FIRST LEARNED about the Apennines in the *World Book Encyclopedia* more than 60 years ago. The set had found a home in my bedroom, and I loved plucking one off the shelf each night for my bedtime reading, randomly opening the volume, and reading whatever caught my fancy. The maps, the photos, and the descriptions opened my eyes to the world. Now here I was, starting into those mountains, the "backbone" of Italy. We would be climbing into and along this range all the way to Assisi—and, if we were going on, all the way to Rome. We were even going to experience a bit of that wind and rain that had "worn them down."

The Way of St. Francis crosses, and occasionally follows, two of the major rivers that drain these mountains: the Arno and the Tiber. The Apennines reminded me in appearance and height of the Blue Ridge mountains near my home in western Virginia. The broad base of their foothills stretches out like fingers into narrow coastal plains.

As at home, we could see springtime progress up the sides of the mountains, as the leaves first broke out along the lower elevations, the darker green giving way to lighter green, then to brown at the top.

~

THE LOOMING CLIMB into those mountains approached, but not before another hour of level and pleasant walking along a blacktop road. No cars passed me, so I had the peaceful, winding lane all to myself. The way was lined with various fir trees, their shade and scents were cool and refreshing, and I felt new energy to pick up my pace, though I imagine that the cappuccino I had consumed with lunch was also helping. I passed ancient olive trees, whose weathered and gnarled trunks spoke of centuries of history in a tough mountain environment. This was the most pleasing stretch of the day, and I was starting to regret that Jane was missing it.

I passed the village of Ferrano. Above its castle and church the evergreen-topped mountains grew closer. Atop a stone wall two men—the first I'd seen in hours—were repairing a grape trellis. I waved to them and then noticed a water spigot conveniently situated on the side of the road marked *potabile*. With a couple of hours of tough climbing ahead, I stopped and quickly downed a half liter and then refilled my bottle and two extras that I had buried in my pack. I knew I was adding a lot of weight ahead of a steep climb, but I was concerned about becoming dehydrated.

I approached a stone bridge over a stream in the fold of the mountain and could see the paved road change to dirt as it turned sharply to the right and uphill. Pulling out my phone, I looked at my GPX tracks and could see that my path indeed turned to the left, upward into the forest. I crossed the bridge, looked down to the stream, and spotted two women, the first pilgrims I'd seen that day. I waved to them and called down a greeting, and they greeted me back, asking "Where are you from?"

"The U.S.," I said, "and you?" *"Deutschland."* We would meet a lot of Germans over the next week, along with Austrians, Swiss, and, of course, Italians.

The women had removed their boots and were soaking their feet in the stream. I could see a third person in their group, a man lying back, his hat covering his eyes. It occurred to me just then that a pause and a short nap might be a good idea, and I pondered for a few moments before resisting the temptation. I waved, shouted *"Auf wiedersehen,"* and *"Buon Cammino"*[5] and turned left onto the dirt mountain road. The toughest part of the day's trek had begun.

It is difficult to find peace and quiet in today's world. Can you remember the last time you heard—nothing?

Dr. Qing Li, *Forest Bathing*

WHAT I FIRST NOTICED AS I plunged into the forest was how steep the road was: just dirt and gravel, with occasional ruts and streaming rivulets. We had trained on mountain roads at home, but this was different. It was steep. Relentlessly steep. A *very tough* climb.

Second, I realized I could no longer "see" the mountains: I was "in" them, surrounded by stands of tall fir trees as far as the eye could see, going ever upward. There was no top, no pass to climb to, just the climb. Just a dirt road, twisting and winding out of view.

The third thing I noticed—and really appreciated at this point—was how cool it was, thanks to those fir trees standing straight, tall, and thick on each side, enveloping me in their shade. After hours in and out of the hot sun, this was a welcome break.

The last thing I noticed was how quiet it was. Silence. Complete silence. No road traffic in the distance. No bird songs, no squirrel chatter. No breeze. Nothing dropping from the trees. No gurgling streams. No other people. Utter silence.

Nothing except the sound of my feet and the "poke-poke" of my poles.

Silence, total silence, is disorienting at first. We are so used to noise that its absence seems odd to us. I can sit home, in total silence, and it is not at all disorienting. But this was silence in an unknown place. I had only a vague idea where I was on the face of the earth. By this point, I reasoned, Jane was up ahead of me in Consuma, our destination for the day. I  looked at my GPX again and figured that I had another hour or two of steep climbing ahead before I reached her.

I also realized, in the silence of the forest, that I was completely alone. I had left the Germans behind. No more vineyards or olive groves, no farmsteads and villas, no more cultivated countryside. The sensual stimulation, the wonder, the delightful novelty in the countryside hours had turned to a steep hillside of straight and tall fir trees.

And silence.

I resisted pulling out my mobile phone, plugging in my headphones, and listening to something, anything, to take away the potent emptiness. I didn't know if this would be the only time I would walk alone (in fact it was), but as odd as it felt, I embraced the enforced silence and the loneliness. The lack of companionship, the lack of sounds, being in a place I didn't know at all—I needed to embrace the gift of strangeness, of complete solitude, the lack of any stimulation—as jarring as it was.

[M]illions of pilgrims are on the move . . . but most often on foot and over considerable distances—for physical hardship remains a definitive aspect of most pilgrimage: arduous passage through the outer landscape prompting subtle exploration of the inner.

Robert Macfarlane, "Rites of Way: Behind the
Pilgrimage Revival

DEPRIVED OF ANY SENSORY STIMULATION, my mind made up for it, sifting through months of random thoughts, as if they had been compressed and the total lack of sensory stimulation released them. At a deep level, I knew I needed this. I knew that this walk, this pilgrimage, would help reorient me after two years of constant pandemic dangers and other stressful news.

Whereas I had regretted that Jane had missed the delightful walk out of Diacceto, I was quite sure now that she had made the right decision. The relentless climb was taxing, and I had no idea—short of looking at my map—how much longer it would go on. I dug my poles in with each step and concentrated. I slowed occasionally to drink water. I decided to resist the temptation to keep looking at my progress; there was nothing to do but enter completely into the moment. I thought about how fortunate I was to be there, to be doing this. I thought back over the previous months—actually the two years of the pandemic—and reminded myself how I had dreamed of these mountains, of the challenges of this climb. It made it all very manageable.

Just when I was really in the "zone"—that moment when I was completely absorbed by the present, by my task of climbing, when I had stopped thinking about the silence and the solitude—I came to a junction. I glanced at my watch and was astonished to realize that I'd been climbing nonstop for an hour. The steep elevation had eased, and then I heard my first sounds. It was the Germans. They appeared below me out of nowhere. How had they come upon me so quickly? My competitive side asserted itself, and I felt a funny urge to stay ahead of them.

Another ten minutes passed. I was staying successfully ahead of the Germans, when a few houses suddenly emerged at a clearing. In front of one of them a man was operating a small backhoe. I knew I was reentering civilization. I decided to stop and drink some water and eat my apple. At that point the Germans caught up to me and stopped to chat. I found out they were from Hanover, that they were heading to Consuma as well. They walked on while I finished my apple.

I CONTINUED along the dirt road, passed a sign telling me that Consuma was still another 45 minutes away[6], and came to a junction where I met the Germans again. They were leaning over a stone wall, studying a map. I knew that the route diverged at this point; a longer option led along a quiet mountain trail into Consuma, and they were choosing that one. The other route—the one I opted to take—turned onto a freshly blacktopped and striped road that hinted at civilization. I waved goodbye to the Germans (it was the last time I would see them) and was suddenly passed by some cyclists coasting fast down the fresh pavement. A cyclist myself, I felt a momentary envy, before I turned uphill toward my destination.

The road was pleasant, and I got lost again in the zone before I decided to check my route. I realized that I had missed a shortcut along a short dirt track and turned back to find it. I left the road, headed upward along a path through a thick stand of pines, and in minutes found myself in the midst of vacation homes. Just then my phone rang. It was Jane. "Are you near Consuma?" she asked, and just at that moment I spied her, directly ahead of me, sitting against a stone wall.

"Turn around and you'll see me."

3

Over the Pass

Pilgrimage Principle 4: Accept whatever is offered to you, as a gift from God.

JANE WAS surprised and delighted to see me. The bus ride into Consuma had indeed taken a mere 20 minutes, as predicted, and, not surprisingly, she had grown restless after waiting three hours for me. Apparently, she had been calling me for the past hour, but my phone had been out of signal range. She was waiting near the vacation homes, about a kilometer from town. She wasn't sure exactly where and when I would arrive and had only guessed that I would come out in this spot. As we walked together down to the busy mountain highway and into town, she filled me in on the brief bus ride and on what she had done in the deserted town while she waited for me. It turned out that everything in Consuma was closed, so Jane hadn't had much to keep her busy. There was no shoulder, and we had to keep close to the guardrail as traffic passed. She was certainly fresher now, maybe just slightly regretting that she had not taken that climb.

"You made the right decision," I said quite sincerely, as I told about the climb through the forest. "For the longest time it was straight uphill. You would have regretted it if you'd come along. It was a killer. I'm serious." Sobered by this, and assured that she'd made the right decision, we entered Consuma together.

CONSUMA IS a small mountain hamlet at 1,050 meters in elevation that sits at the saddle between the Casentino region and Pontassieve, known as the Passo della Consuma. Since the late Middle Ages, it had been a legendary stop for travelers between the regions, but like most communities in the mountains, it is lightly populated today, full instead of holiday and vacation homes.

We had tried to find a place to stay here before we left Florence, but being the Wednesday before Easter, we had been unable to find a vacancy. Elena, who with her husband Luca ran a B&B in town, offered us instead a room in their *rifugio* on the lower level of their home, in an even smaller settlement simply called Villa, about seven kilometers beyond Consuma. With no other choices and, following our pilgrim tradition of receiving whatever was offered to us, we gladly accepted her invitation, even though we thought we would be going well off our route. However, it turned out to be an excellent opportunity.

Consuma was still quiet when we arrived, with only a small café open. We phoned Elena, who said that she'd be there in a few minutes. Ironically, she had just picked up her children from school, back in Pontassieve. We sat at a table outside a shuttered restaurant while we waited for her to arrive. A refreshing mountain breeze blew down the street, and, cooling down from the long climb, I pulled on another layer. I put up my feet, and for the first time in hours realized just how tired I was.

Before I could get too comfortable, however, Elena arrived and we piled our packs into the back of her small station wagon and slipped in next to her smiling and curious children as she drove us on the winding road down from the pass to their home, the Rifugio di San Jacopo in Villa.

Rifgugio San Jacopo, Villa

Villa is an ancient village, with a recorded history going back about a thousand years; today it is just a few homes with a dozen inhabitants, but it had been more prosperous in the 16th century, boasting a population of 330. Luca and Elena's house had been in Luca's family "forever" as he told me; his uncle had been the parish priest. He and Elena relocated here in recent years in order to give their children a rural upbringing and to be able to connect with the pilgrim community that passes through here.[1] There is a record of the church, the Chiesa San Jacopo, that dates to the 11th century, but it had been rebuilt in the 16th century and renovated recently (led by Luca, who is an architect). We took time to go inside and admire the beautiful white plaster walls and the typical raftered roof, well-lit by two windows at the front.

As I looked out behind this property, I felt like I could be back home in the Allegheny Mountains. Luca and Elena's small homestead with about an acre of cultivated garden and fenced pasture was guarded by two friendly "working dogs" who kept watch over a flock of honking geese. (Luca told us that wild boars are still around and showed us a skull from one.) Fruit tree blossoms waved in a gentle, cool breeze on the hillside. In their own small way they were helping to reverse the outward migration from these mountains that had slowly drained the population for centuries. I could sense the satisfaction in his voice as he talked about this place, his ancient family home, and how they were once again working the land. Next to him, ancient terraces of the adjoining farmstead faintly hinted at the long history of this place.

We showered and washed clothes while Luca lit a fire in the common room. The warmth of the fire matched the warmth of their hospitality. For our supper Elena prepared a homemade genuinely Tuscan meal: four courses, probably the finest meal we have ever eaten in Italy. (We were starving

—the last time we'd eaten was in Diacceto, 900 meters of climbing and six hours before—and nothing had been open in Consuma!) Luca came downstairs during the last course, the *dolce* (dessert) and talked to us at length about the ancient history of the region, his family's history in the village, and how he had come here frequently as a child. He told us about his work with a local association of the Way of St. Francis in Tuscany and how he and Elena appreciate meeting people who have, as he said, "An appreciation for the Franciscan approach to life." He also emphasized, "We also want to contribute personally to a different way of life where nature, human connections, and a different kind of economy can be experienced."

The hospitality, the time our hosts took to talk with us and hear from us, the spirit in which they approach their work—that is the kind of connection that we had hoped to find on this journey and is indeed one of the reasons we go on pilgrimage, which is at its heart different from simply being "tourists." Because we had kept our plans flexible and adaptable (see Pilgrimage Principle 6), we had been led to this experience and these people. Luca helped us out in one more significant way: He told us that his cousin had a B&B in Stia, the next town along the Way, and offered to phone ahead and make a reservation for us. We thanked him and heartily agreed. Having our host phone ahead saved us both time and communication challenges since his cousin spoke no English.[2]

After a good night's sleep and an excellent breakfast, Elena offered to drive us back to Consuma, but at this point I wondered, *Why would we do that? Couldn't we just climb the ridge across from their home and continue onward to Stia?* It would shave seven kilometers off our day, at least two hours of walking and several hill climbs. Thinking ahead on all the climbing we had before us in the coming days, we decided that there was nothing to gain from going backward; we would have plenty of hills ahead to climb. While I had an informal goal of walking the entire route, at this point I realized there was no compelling reason to do so. We would choose an easier day that was being offered to us and be thankful for it.[3]

Luca and Elena and their children

After settling our bill, we said farewell to Luca and Elena, crossed the road, and followed a path into the woods, which vanished after 50 meters. We backtracked, moved sideways along the hills, then bushwhacked our way upward and soon found our route and the familiar Tau markers painted on a tree trunk at the top of the ridge.

The yellow Tau or capital T is the universal symbol of the Way of St. Francis. Along with a blue and yellow blaze, it marks the entire route from Florence to Rome. Its significance is ancient—going back to the Hebrew prophet Ezekiel and continuing through the Christian era when a cross—also signifying the crucifixion of Christ—came to be a universal identifier of the faithful. Francis, according to his first biographer, Thomas of Celano, marked the back of his tunic and his monk's habit with the Tau as a way to identify the wearer as a member of a religious order. He even signed his letters with it and occasionally carved it or painted it onto the walls of some of the sanctuaries he established. Similar to the yellow arrow or scallop shell that mark both the route and the pilgrim along the Camino de Santiago, the Tau cross identifies both along the Way of St. Francis.

IT WAS A GORGEOUS, sunny day as we followed the ridge eastward. The top of the ridge was still barren; the leafy path was dotted with delightful patches of yellow primrose. We passed the Castle Castagnaio (which has been guarding this spot for a thousand years) and then descended to the Arno River, which had been a mighty flume when we saw it in Florence. We were now just a few kilometers from its source, and it was narrow and shallow enough to wade across, if we'd wanted that.

The area we had now entered was steeped in history. In addition to several castles, there are ancient Roman sites and sacred sites of the even-more-ancient Etruscans going back three thousand years.

WE CROSSED THE RIVER, and after a brief walk along a highway found a pleasant gravel path into Stia, passing by several millraces, evidence of the ancient mills that had made this a significant place in the Middle Ages. The western slopes of the Apennines were famed for their wool and woven cloth. Their abundance—and surpluses—had played a role in the prosperity of Tuscany and in the rise of Italian banking during the 14th century.

The short and easy day felt more like a stroll than a hike, and we soon entered the center of Stia with its elongated, arcaded square, lined with three-story stone buildings. We found our B&B, and though Luca's cousin spoke very little English, she found a way to tell us that we ought to head down to the Trattoria Falterona next door for a meal since it would be closing in an hour.

Central Piazza, Stia

Italians tend to eat their bigger meal of the day at noon. Restaurants typically open between 11:00 and 2:00, the midday hour. A *ristorante* will have a more sophisticated menu and may cost more. A *trattoria* or *osteria*, both family-owned restaurants, serve simpler, traditional food, and that's where we found ourselves.

By now it was a warm afternoon, and we found a table under a large awning. We were tired, thirsty, and hungry but deeply satisfied after our easy day. Families sat at larger tables nearby, deep in conversation. Behind them sat a group of four younger men; one was vaping and another smoking. The odor wafted our way, annoying me. Jane also noticed this. I eyed a table farther toward the edge of the patio, leaned over the table, and suggested quietly, "Maybe we ought to move to that table over there." Jane looked that way, but just then the server approached, leaned over the table, pulled out a pencil from behind her ear and a small spiral note pad, and asked us (in Italian) what we wanted.

I shook my head and asked, *"Il menu?"* She waved her hands (indicating there was no menu) and started to explain, in Italian, what our choices were for the day. I needed her to realize that we didn't understand and said in Italian that we didn't speak the language: *"Non capisco, non parlo italiano."* This was a key phrase that I had memorized, but it was to no avail. She kept on speaking in Italian, calm and friendly, but it was clear we were going nowhere.

Just then the vaper jumped out of his seat and came to my rescue. In excellent English he explained what she was trying to tell us: We could choose one of several pastas, one of which was ravioli. He told me that there was no menu, but we could choose our pasta with whatever sauce we wanted, and we selected the ravioli with red, or *rosso*, sauce. With his help, I was also able to order two salads, *insalati*, and some drinks: *birra, acqua frizzante,* and *vino bianco.* The server nodded, wrote it in her notebook, smiled, and walked away. Humbled, I thanked the young man, embarrassed about how I had misjudged him. Minutes later the server appeared with my beer, a liter bottle of sparkling water, and a bottle of white wine, which she proceeded to uncork. Jane stared at it in disbelief; she had thought she was just getting a small *glass* of wine. We laughed. This was an authentic Italian *trattoria*, and the server probably thought nothing of the two of us drinking a whole bottle on top of the bottle of beer. In the end, most of the bottle went home to our host.

4

Into the Forest

Draw the resilience you will need from those who have preceded you, for pilgrims are a hardy breed. They trudge rough roads, put in long days and live on bread crusts. But hunger turns those crusts into gourmet fare and pilgrims sleep well from their fatigue, even when their beds are hard ground and stones are their pillows.

Huston Smith, Foreword, to *The Art of Pilgrimage*

THE NEXT MORNING Jane and I stood at the counter of a small café on the edge of Stia, sipping a cappuccino and eating a light breakfast of yogurt and pastries. This was going to be another beautiful day, with bright blue skies and moderate temperatures, perfect for a trek. I studied a map and tried to pronounce the names of the towns and villages that we were about to walk through over the next three days. We picked out sandwiches for lunch from the display case since there would be no grocery stores or cafés ahead of us that day. We were about to begin our ascent into the Casentino Forest National Park.

I was both excited and apprehensive. Our ultimate destination, deep in the forest, was La Verna, one of the most visited and popular of Francis's sanctuaries. I was excited for the history and beauty of the trek ahead. We would be experiencing what is possibly the most mystical part of the route, as we dove deep into the Casentino. We would be passing the monastery and hermitage of Camaldoli, a spiritual center that, remarkably, had been operating continuously for a thousand years.

My apprehension was about the steep rocky tracks, the rain-swelled streams, the unknown, the sheer remoteness and wildness of it all. The distance from Stia to La Verna was 43 kilometers, and we planned on three days to get there. But my main worry was the elevation: We would be climbing nearly 3,000 meters over those 43 kilometers, crossing at least three mountain passes before the final—and most difficult—ascent to La Verna itself. It would be similar to our second day, to Consuma, but times three.

Pilgrimage Principle 6: Keep flexible plans and adapt as you go.

WE HAD PLANNED flexibility into this stretch. We would walk as far as we felt able to each day and make our lodging plans "on the go." This created some risk, since we could never be certain what might be open. For example, we had hoped to get as far as Camaldoli that day, where we had hoped to stay in *La Foresteria*,[1] the monastery's guest quarters, but it was full of tourists and other day hikers, as were the two other hotels in town. Instead, we picked a place recommended by our guidebook, Rifugio Asqua,[2] an isolated hostel in the mountains, five kilometers before Camaldoli. Our willingness to be flexible would allow the journey to unfold however it did.

I closed my guidebook, looked at Jane, and said, "Okay, only 12 kilometers and only 600 meters. We can do this." We were now several days into our pilgrimage. Jane was over her jet lag and said to me, "Let's go. I feel ready."

The initial climb out of Stia was beautiful. The first two hours to the village of Lonnano were under an infinite blue sky, with the vistas widening over the valley of the Arno. The towns of Stia and Pratovecchio to its south were spread out below us as we climbed ever higher. We took an easy pace; our relatively short distance that day meant we need not hurry. We passed a young couple from Germany walking with their small dog, who was taking its time.

Two friendly Italian Sheep dogs outside Lonnano

FOREST IS an ambiguous term for Americans. We typically think of any stand of woodland as a forest, but we also have our own formally designated national forests. We tend to think of some national forests as wild, unknown places, or at least as wild as it gets in the United States, where our recorded history is only a few centuries old.

In Europe a forest is more a place of cultivation; in England, the forests were originally hunting reserves for nobility. To understand the European forest we need to think of it as more like a preserve. The Casentino has a long history, going back nearly three thousand years, back to the Etruscans who first settled and left traces of their culture there. Over the past millennium, the Casentino has been cultivated for its timber, with large stands of fir trees planted in rows, alongside the native beech, oak, and chestnut. The monks who inhabit Camaldoli have been stewards of that forest now for ten centuries.

ON OUR WAY to Asqua we wound our way in and out of the woodland and along narrow paths through steep ravines, while stepping carefully over shallow streams. This was an ancient track, and we passed overgrown farmsteads, abandoned stone houses, and ancient, overgrown retaining walls. We paused for lunch at a spot on the edge of a steep ravine where, through the still budding branches, we could see all the way back to Lonnano. The bunches of primroses, which I had first noticed two days before, were now everywhere around us, popping up through the decaying leaves and patches of pine needles.

In the very early afternoon, we passed more farms and *agriturismo*—farms that hosts guests and provides meals, often produce from their own operation—and passed rows of fenced pastures, some containing pigs, knee deep in the mud. We passed more flocks of sheep with the large (and largely friendly) Italian sheepdogs watching over them. We saw more hikers going in both directions, including a large group of Italian teens with heavy packs who must have been camping. Shortly before Asqua, we plunged for the last time into the thick of the forest, all the while on a gentle climb.

Rifugio Asqua

The fierce wind drying our clothes at Asqua

• • •

RIFUGIO ASQUA CAME as an unexpected and welcome sight in the midst of a dense stand of fir, like a mirage, except it was real. This type of mountain hostel, with clean and warm dormitories and three meals a day, is common in Europe but a rarity for Americans. Our friendly host, Sabrina, offered to wash our clothes in her machine, and we gladly accepted; it gave us a chance to shower and nap. We hung our clothes out just as the wind picked up, roaring like thunder. It was difficult to get things onto the line before they blew away, but they were dry in less than half an hour, blown horizontally by the great gusts.

The first and easiest of our three days of climbing was over, and we felt encouraged. We had the rest of the long afternoon to nap, write leisurely about our experiences, and plan for the coming days by reviewing our lodging options. We had one of the dorms to ourselves that night but not before we were fed a sumptuous four-course meal, cooked by Sabrina's mother, that closely rivaled what we had been fed by Elena back in Villa.

In ancient forests . . . there are no atheists.

Bill McKibben, *The Age of Missing Information*

THE NEXT MORNING we downed a small Italian breakfast (toast, pastries, and coffee) before we headed out toward Camaldoli, five kilometers away, where we had originally hoped to stay the night. There we hoped to catch a "second" breakfast, before a steep climb through the mountains. The walk through the deep forest was along a wide jeep track, climbing gently 300 meters before a long and sharp descent into Camaldoli itself. The wind continued, though it diminished as we descended.

Camaldoli convent

The Camaldoli convent lies at the bottom of a deep ravine; its hermitage sits three kilometers up a very steep mountain. The monks of these two monasteries have preserved and cultivated this remote, Eden-like retreat continually since its founding by Saint Romuald in 1012, on lands given him by Count Maldolo[3] two centuries before Francis. (I wondered whether Francis had passed through here in his time.) It is not common in Western Europe to find a monastery that has such a continual existence; one mostly finds the ruins of these great places. Camaldoli is also exceptional in that it was a meeting place between the East and the West, the Byzantine and the Roman church traditions, resulting in its own beautiful synthesis. The monks of Camaldoli had actually introduced the firs that grew so abundantly in these mountains, and they still cultivate traditional medicinal herbs that they sell in the pharmacy next to the church.

It was the day before Easter and there were crowds even at mid-morning. We stopped in a café for sandwiches, tea, and cappuccino. Except for the cars and the bicycles whizzing by, and the fact that the place was crawling with tourists, it felt like time stood still here. We could easily imagine this place several hundred years ago, deep in the folds of the gorge and looking as peaceful as its gentle stream. I took a mental note to spend more time here next time I walked this route.

THE NEXT SECTION of our hike would be as difficult as we had imagined, and we left our options open from the outset. We knew that there was an open room in a hotel in Badia Prataglia, over the first mountain and after another three hours of walking. But we knew that if we had the energy, a better option was to continue all the way to Santicchio, another guest house a further nine kilometers over yet another mountain. If we could get there, we would give ourselves a shorter day of climbing to La Verna on Easter Sunday. If we made it to Santicchio, we would have climbed 1,500 meters in elevation over roughly 17 kilometers.

We set off from the monastery but immediately found our path confusing. The marked route out of town—a modest climb along the edge of the gorge—was closed. A landslide had blocked it. We headed farther down the road before finding our "detour," which was a steep dirt track that led upward at a ridiculously steep 45-degree angle. We stared in disbelief at it for a minute. "They have to be kidding. This looks nearly impossible," I said to Jane. Just at that moment the German couple with the small dog appeared, and I could see the same disbelief on their faces as they peered upward. The dog sat down; it was clearly going to be difficult to coax it up this steep embankment, so the man bent over, picked it up, and started climbing slowly.

Jane looked sideways at me. "That looks like a good idea. You want to carry me up?" We both laughed, leaned into our poles, and started the climb.

> The object of pilgrimage is not rest and recreation—to get away from it all. To set out on a pilgrimage is to throw down the challenge to everyday life.
>
> Huston Smith, *The Art of Pilgrimage*

THE NEXT CLIMB over the mountain was indeed hard, but the steep grade eased a bit after half an hour and the exceeding beauty made it difficult to complain. We had left Asqua wearing our light winter coats, but after all that climbing we were down to short sleeves and shorts. The thunderous wind was haunting and distracted us from fatigue. We passed massive fir trees a hundred feet high that tipped to the side, leaning over the path as we trekked below them. We passed mountain huts. Groups of mountain bikers passed us, politely calling or ringing bells well in advance of reaching us. Near the top of the mountain, we passed stands of broom interspersed with beeches, their wide, sweeping branches ready to embrace us should the wind try to whisk us off.

The energy from our late breakfast powered us through, and we made it to Badia Prataglia in three more hours. It was now 2:00, early afternoon, but we were very tired, having just walked and climbed over a mountain, the toughest and longest segment so far for either of us. We planned to stop, get lunch, and see if we felt like going any farther.

Badia Prataglia is a very beautiful resort town, nestled deep in a pocket surrounded on all sides by the mountains. It was once a monastery (the name means "monastery in the meadow"). Today all that remains of that monastery is a parish church from the 10th century atop an even more ancient crypt. Once a center for timber, it is now popular with hikers and bikers, its hills covered with vacation homes.

The central *piazza* had a lovely, covered pavilion that we thought would make a great spot for a picnic lunch, but the grocery store where we hoped to buy that lunch was closed. I deduced that we had arrived at the *riposo*, the rest time. We headed instead to a café in the center of town, where we bought sandwiches, cappuccinos, and pastries. After a rest, I asked Jane what she thought we ought to do next.

"Let's push on," she said, then finished her cappuccino and gathered her pack. From Asqua we had walked 14 kilometers *and* climbed nearly 900 meters. Ahead lay *another mountain*, a smaller ridge after that: a total of 9 kilometers and 600 meters more to ascend; it would take us at least three hours.

She had thrown down the challenge and I was impressed.

"Are you positive you want to continue?" I asked, just to make sure. She nodded yes and that was it.

We pulled on our packs, grabbed our poles, and in 10 minutes we were at the edge of town, where we walked a nice grassy path and then up a very steep, very loose, and very rocky grade. A lot of rainwater had gushed down this path over years and cut deep ruts. Stepping carefully along the edges of the gullies, I led upward on the single-file path, alerting Jane to the sturdiest footing.

The view back to Badia Prataglia

Yet, as difficult as it was, it could not have been more beautiful, even with the stiff wind. I forgot about how tired I was feeling. The stunning vista back down to Badia Prataglia—in continual view as we climbed—was worth every ounce of effort, and the views got better and better the higher we ascended. The short, steep, nearby peaks were topped with a patchwork of dark fir stands and light green pastures. With each succeeding vista more spectacular than the previous one, I suddenly felt small, humbled by both the landscape and the physical effort it was taking to cross it. I was understanding more and more why Francis chose mountain sanctuaries, particularly with wide vistas, as places of retreat.

We soon topped out the climb and followed an easy grade along the ridgetop. Up high on the mountain, the wind roared stronger and the trees leaned, though there was little left of them; nearly all the treetops had been snapped, as if a giant swinging a sickle had lopped them off. Occasionally a tree had fallen across our path, but this fierce gale was under the most gorgeous blue sky and kept us cool as we walked.

We walked through this battered forest for nearly an hour before we descended into the lovely mountain village of Frassineta. Even though we were heading downhill, the downed trees and occasional rocky and uneven surface of the path required us to exercise constant vigilance. This was the hardest part of a long and demanding hike, the final kilometers. The mental and physical fatigue tested our resilience. Jane had been relieving hers by listening to podcasts, finding the distraction helpful over these last long stretches, keeping her from ruminating about how much farther we had to go. I didn't want to be distracted at that point; I listened to the roar of the wind through the trees

Frassineta

Frassineta, like many villages that we had passed through, was inhabited, indicated by open shutters and parked cars, but we saw no one and pushed on through. By now it was late afternoon, our shadows were lengthening behind us, and the sun was sinking lower. I guessed we had at least another two hours of light left, and we paused to look at a route marker that indicated Santicchio was still 50 minutes away. I slowed to take photos, but Jane charged ahead, imagining a comforting shower and a hot meal.

It was also here that we saw the first route signs for the

ancient Via Romea Germanica,[4] one of the many routes that converge in this part of the Casentino as we neared La Verna. The sky was a deeper blue, the wind continued its deafening roar, but the evening was coming on fast. I ran on sheer determination for the last half hour as the path became narrower, and rougher, the closer we got to our goal.

Around 6:00 Santicchio came into view, and it was a welcome sight. An ancient farmstead with several buildings, it had thick walls and a friendly dog that greeted us as we closed in.

Rarely have a hot shower and a bed felt so welcome, and for once we were glad for the late Italian supper hour; we needed a good rest, even this late in the day. I had experienced this type of complete fatigue before—mental, physical, and emotional—which is paradoxically very satisfying. I reflected later that on all our walks together, this had been perhaps the hardest. Whatever lingering fear of "wimpiness" Jane might have started the day with, she had driven it out on this leg. That night we had definitely earned the bed, the meal, and the relaxing evening.

The final kilometer to Santicchio

5

Brother Wind, Sister Water

We praise you, Lord, for Brothers Wind and Air
fair and stormy, in all weather's moods
by which you cherish all that you have made.

We praise you, Lord, for Sister Water,
so useful, humble, precious and pure.

St. Francis of Assisi, "Canticle of the Sun"

IN SPITE of the thick stone walls of the ancient B&B, we heard the wind howl for the second straight night. It was Easter morning. We ate breakfast with an American/Italian couple and their two sons before they took off in their car for a day of hiking in Badia Prataglia or Camaldoli—they weren't sure which. We shared that we were off for our last and steepest climb yet, to La Verna "just" seven to eight kilometers away but 720 meters of elevation.

We were in for a day of stark, raw beauty from the moment we headed out the door. The day before had been sunshine, sweat, and short sleeves; today we layered up under our warm coats, and donned hiking shoes. Fortunately, the weather forecast did not predict rain, but the sky was a mixture of blue and white patches, interspersed with billows of heavy granite-colored clouds blown swiftly across the sky. They matched the color of the surrounding rocky outcrops, as if the wind had carved them out of the surrounding mountains and was scattering them across the sky.

The wind, our constant, noisy companion for the previous two days, now felt familial: Brother Wind.

Rimbocci

FRANCIS IS CREDITED with writing the first extant poem in Italian. The *Laudes Creaturarum*, "Praise of the Creatures," is affectionately called the "Canticle of the Sun."[1] Before it, all poems, theology, and other literary works were written in Latin. This ancient language had remained the official lingua franca, or international language, of Italy, but no one spoke it, least of all the common person. It was the language of the educated, and it was only used in writing. It was in keeping with Francis that everything he communicated should be accessible to the most unlearned. So naturally he would put his delight in all of God's creation into the vernacular. The verse celebrated not just creatures, but the sun and moon, even wind and water. To him they were personal, and he spoke of them affectionately, familiarly, as "Brother Sun, Sister Moon." He referred to all creation as "Sister/Mother Earth." For Francis, life was to be celebrated in its entirety, including the difficult or fearful: Even the end of our lives was known to him as "Sister Bodily Death." The world and all it contained was not a stranger or antagonist, but a vast community, family, that nurtured all. For Francis, life and all that it contained was a celebration.

I THOUGHT of this as we headed downhill, buffeted by Brother Wind. I had never experienced such a wind so continually and for so long. We heard it, we felt it: a fierce gale, punishing, persistent, loud. It quieted as we descended into the valley but rose again as we headed back into the heights.

To the southeast, we could see Poggio Montopoli,[2] our first summit on our way to La Verna. Above and beyond Poggio Montopoli we glimpsed La Verna itself, one of the most sacred places along the whole Way of St. Francis, if not in all of Italy.

"Continue downhill on the eroded and sometimes slippery path," the guidebook advised. Since it was Easter morning, we hoped to be at our destination by early after-noon, but first we had to walk for about 45 minutes to the village of Rimbocchi, deep in the folds of the surrounding peaks, where we came to a stream crossing. This meant a loss of over 150 meters, all of which we were going to have to regain as soon as we crossed.

I was envisioning a celebration as we entered this village, it being Easter, but the place was eerily quiet. I wasn't surprised that the pizzeria was closed, but so was everything else: every door and every shutter. There were no church bells, no cars moving. Where was everyone?

We knew from a sign that La Verna was 18 kilometers away via the paved road. We were instead taking the "direct" route—only five kilometers, but straight up the mountain.

We walked through the village, crossed a highway, and found the trail sign that pointed across a wide stream at the base of the mountain. My guidebook said, "Cross the creek on stones," but it was not going to be possible that day. Sister Water was fierce this spring morning: Those stones were under more than a foot of swift-moving, icy water. I wasn't at all sure how deep it might be in the middle, and I wasn't sure of the footing.

"No way I'm walking through that," Jane said.

I imagined that there must be another shallow spot for crossing the stream or maybe even a log bridge and, using my walking poles to thrash the underbrush, I started walking upstream on a futile search while Jane took to the road to see if there was another bridge or ford close by.

We wasted the next 20 minutes searching. I knew from my guidebook that there was a car bridge a few kilometers upstream, but that seemed a long detour. I resigned myself to the fact that there was nothing to do but ford the stream.

That's when we were surprised by a young woman suddenly appearing out of the brush downstream. She introduced herself: She was German, had left La Verna that morning (she must have left *very* early!), and was on her way to Florence. She pointed with her hiking pole to a spot about 20 meters downstream. "It's shallower there, and you can wade across safely."

We were incredulous. Where had she come from? Why hadn't we spotted her? Why hadn't we heard her snapping twigs and crunching on the dry leaves along the stream bank as she bushwhacked her way along it? It was too mysterious. We hadn't seen a soul in the hour since we'd left Santicchio. We hadn't seen or heard her on the opposite bank or coming down the trail. Furthermore, it was peculiar to meet a pilgrim walking in the opposite direction; in fact, she was the only one we met on our entire trek who was walking north toward Florence. And she appeared just when we needed someone. Perhaps she was some kind of mysterious Cammino Angel, sent to show us the way?

Whatever she was, we thanked her, then headed where she had pointed, still slightly baffled by the encounter. Sitting on some rocks, we slipped off our shoes, pulled on our sandals, and waded across carefully. The water was swift and cold, *very* cold. The bottom seemed uneven at first, and so I stepped carefully and made sure to keep my balance with my poles—I didn't want to slip and tumble with my pack on. In the end the footing was firm, and we were both across in minutes. We dried our feet with a small towel and then were on our way, gradually and then very steeply upward, still wondering about the encounter. The young woman remained the only person we encountered that *entire day*, until we reached La Verna three hours later.

IF THE WAY OF ST. Francis is partly about understanding the challenges of the elements, this section embodies it more than any other. Brother Rock and Sister Dirt accompanied us as we steadily, relentlessly climbed for the third day in a row. Unlike previous days, however, there would be no descents. This is often described as the most difficult of all the climbs on this part of the Way, and we were glad we were going to make a short day of it. At times the pathway became bare, tilted rock with occasional scree, or loose stone. Being early spring, the trees were largely without leaf, and we were rewarded with breathtaking views back down the valley towards Rimbocchi, and even across the valley to Santicchio. Brother Wind, who had quieted as we descended into the valley, now dialed up with each meter that we ascended. To add to the challenge, I grew hungrier with each step, and the combination of the wind and fatigue quieted us both, especially me.

After crossing just below the top of Poggio Montopoli, we were presented with the full view of Monte Penna, home of La Verna, with its distinctive, mesa-like profile. I could see why Francis was drawn to this place. I also recognized how a person in the Middle Ages, walking without a map, would be able to navigate using only such sights as a reference. The leafless trees barely obscured the mountaintop. I kept trying to make out the monastery, which I knew to be up there somewhere, but in Italy it is often difficult to distinguish between where the mountain ends and the stone structures begin. After another 10 minutes along a muddy jeep trail, we crossed an asphalt road and found ourselves entering the deep, mysterious beechwood that is part of the lore and mystique of La Verna.

Monte Penna

This section of old-growth forest and moss-covered rock was a welcome sensory feast. The forest floor, carpeted with brown leaves, was coming awake everywhere in green shoots, bunches of yellow primroses, and other blue and lavender wildflowers. The fallen timbers were covered with moss. The rotting trees were returning to the soil, nourishing the new life. The wind was quieter now, and the air was deeply scented with this rich cycle of decay emerging into new life. This alone was worth the day's climb, and the effort of the previous two hours was forgotten.

The boulders grew in size, as did the stands of the trees. Without the wind, the mossy covering muted even the sound of our steps. We walked on, absorbed in the quiet and mystery. Jane stopped frequently to take photos; I could see that she was mesmerized. "I feel as if I'm in a fairytale. Or maybe the *Wizard of Oz*," she said.

The mysterious Beechwood

We walked on in quiet wonder, the path snaking around the giant boulders, the deepest and thickest mass of them known as *La Ghiaccaia* (The Icebox), where the caves were once used to preserve and keep food cool. I also found out later that these mysterious woods—before the arrival of the

Franciscans—had harbored thieves who used the same jumbled maze of rocks as hideouts.

The Icebox

The path broadened and the boulders receded, giving way to even taller beeches. We were now walking along a gentle slope, the mountain occasionally obscured, then revealing itself in jagged pinnacles emerging out of the forest floor, which had become a thick carpet of bluebells and ferns. Still climbing gently upward. I stopped frequently to take photos, and Jane got way ahead of me. I had forgotten about my hunger.

The path curved, and then the cliff face—20 or 30 meters high—came into view. Our path followed along its base, but we both stopped and just stared, then pulled out our phones for more pictures. The buildings of the monastery rose dramatically above the cliff, as if they had been chiseled directly out of the rock.

At this point the path cut across a green meadow, but we walked with our heads cocked upward and to our left, mesmerized by the sight above our heads. I now understood why this place drew so many visitors from around the world every year.

The dirt path ended abruptly at a stone wall and gate-house. A set of steps led around the gate, and we scrambled up and over. Turning to our left, we saw the final climb of the day: a very steep stone-paved path (it felt like a ramp) leading upward for about 100 meters. In his last visit here in 1224, Francis had been so weakened by illness that a donkey was employed to carry him up to the top.

After climbing all day, we were eager to reach the finish. We were, or at least I was, very hungry. And thirsty. The climb had taken a lot longer than I'd anticipated, and while I'd been entranced by the beech forest, my stomach now reminded me of how ravenous I was. Jane paused as she reached the ramp.

"You're kidding me," she said, looking up at it with incredulity (though by now this sort of thing had become quite common). "We still have to climb *that*?"

"Yup," I said, "but then we're at the end." We'd met Sister Water earlier, and now that we were out of the beech-wood Brother Wind returned. Up ahead of us were still Brothers Fatigue and Hunger, as well as Sister Thirst, but with the same determination that I'd seen in her face the day before, Jane took off on one last climb up the last member of our family: Sister Mountain.

6

That Rock 'Twixt Tiber and the Arno

On the rude rock 'twixt Tiber and the Arno
From Christ did he receive the final seal,
Which during two whole years his members bore

-Dante Alligheri, *Paradiso*

Regardless of what the hermitages are now, they were life-lines for Francis. Always frail, he needed time to recover both spiritually and physically from his far-ranging preaching tours. His friars, too, needed solitude and contemplation. The Franciscans spent so much time on the road that they required retreats along the way for cama-raderie and spiritual renewal.

Linda Bird Francke, *On the Road with Francis of Assisi*

LA VERNA, sitting at an elevation of 1,300 meters on a pronounced rocky outcrop of Monte Penna, was an ancient place of worship, where in antiquity the Romans venerated Laverna, the goddess of thieves. By the late Middle Ages, Count Orlando of Chiusi owned the entire mountaintop. He was so moved after hearing Francis preach at a wedding feast that he offered him the mountaintop as a retreat. Francis had already established a rule that neither he nor his followers could own property, but contrary to this principle he accepted, and it became one of his most beloved sanctuaries and ultimately the most famous.

When we made our final ascent to the top of the cliff, which the great Italian poet Dante had called "the rude rock 'twixt Tiber and the Arno," and saw the stunning, sweeping vista over those same two river valleys, we understood immediately why Francis loved the place—the view from the heights affords a unique perspective on the world. Francis frequently chose clifftops, especially with caves and crevices, as sanctuaries. In his time, the site would have been modest: small wooden huts and a small stone chapel built above a particularly dramatic natural feature—a deep fissure in the rock with an overhang for a roof, the *sasso spicco*[1]—where Francis liked to withdraw to pray. Besides allowing him a place to escape crowds and find much-needed solitude, this place was cooler during the hot Italian summers.

It was here, in the last years of his life, that he supposedly received the stigmata—the wounds of Christ. There is a Chapel of the Stigmata built upon the site, but there are also two other churches, a Franciscan monastery and a large *foresta* (guesthouse) with rooms for hundreds. When we arrived it was Easter Day and La Verna had lots of visitors —it receives a million per year—who came to worship and to hike the peaceful deep green woodlands above.

Brother Wind was still our fast companion when we arrived, and he shrieked through the narrow tunnels between the myriad buildings. Once we checked in, we headed inside to warm up and take showers in our bright, modern room with twin beds. We were as relieved to be out of the taxing, constant wind as we were to be done climbing. We congratulated each other on our achievement: The most taxing climbs were behind us—seven mountains, a hundred kilometers, over 5,000 meters in elevation. From here on it would be easier. We had reached the literal and figurative high point of our walk.

La Foresta, or guest hotel

Dinner was served at seven, so we spent our time peering into the church and chapels. It was too cold and windy to comfortably walk the grounds. Besides, it was getting dark and fatigue was catching up with us. Still, as I looked to the forest above I could see that this place was worth devoting more time to, and I made a note to myself to one day return to walk the trails above the sanctuary and take in the peace and solitude that must still exist there.

The busy, hotel-like atmosphere masked slightly the beauty and mystery of this place. The clockwork schedule of meals in the large dining room and the curt, but polite, dining and front desk staff were reminders that this was as much a destination visited by busloads of tourists coming to walk through the churches and chapels as it was a destination for pilgrims—like us—arriving on foot.

Looking south towards the Tiber Valley

WITH ITS LEGENDS and dramatic setting, La Verna blends together all the inspiration, mystery, and contradictions of

Saint Francis. He had chosen a life of total poverty, dedi-
cating his energy to preaching and serving the poor, but he
didn't stop there. He was hard on his body, performing
frequent long fasts and enduring cold and extreme weather,
often clothed in little more than his tunic. He often gave
away the very cloak that kept him warm, and he slept
directly on the ground or on rock.

He was so hard on himself that in the last years of his
life he was perpetually ailing, which curtailed his ministry.
Exactly why he chose to be this way is open to speculation.
His biographers, both medieval and modern, suggest that it
was in penance for his licentious past and as an example to
others in a world of ostentatious wealth and power. He also
had a frail body to begin with, and his imprisonment in
Perugia as a younger man may have left him with lifelong
illnesses, such as malaria. In stories about their lives, saints
always appear to be hard on their bodies, which seems to be
a requirement, their stories often embellished to the point
that it is difficult to distinguish between fact and exaggera-
tion. This is true with Francis, though there is no doubt that
enough of it was true; he admitted toward the end of his life
that he had been too hard on his "Brother Body."

The stigmata supposedly appeared on Francis during a
40-day fast in 1224, two years before his death. He received
five wounds—one on each hand and foot and one on his
side—similar to the wounds of Christ. This is likely the first
recorded instance of this in history.[2] They were reportedly
painful and debilitating, but he hid them under bandages,
and they were reportedly not seen until after his death when
a number of witnesses attested to them.

I knew about the stigmata long before I arrived at La
Verna, and I spent time contemplating their meaning as I
walked down a long, covered corridor that leads from the

Basilica of Our Lady of the Assumption to the Chapel of the Stigmata.

Ever since the first reports of them—a few years after his death—they have been a subject of skepticism and controversy. Modern biographers are dubious about the divine origin of these wounds, suggesting that they were the result of some other disease or illness, and many doubting that they occurred at all. Yet his later medieval biographers were not in doubt, nor are many of the million faithful who come here each year to visit.

Chapel of Our Lady of the Angels and the basilica across Sundial Square

Hagiography—stories and biographies of saints, martyrs, and other venerated persons—were written to encourage the faithful to emulate them. All the saints had miracles attributed to them. Miracles are a requirement for canonization—the more the better—and this is true with

Francis. I am personally dubious about many, perhaps most, but I do not doubt that some of them were true.[3] But the miracle of the stigmata baffles me the most. I wrestle not so much with the "what" or "how" or even the truth of them but more the "why." Why would he want them in the first place? Why would a man who celebrated and loved beauty and life so much want debilitating wounds on his body? Why would a loving God give them? I puzzled about this as I walked along the corridor toward the chapel that commemorates them and looked at the cycle of frescoes that depict the episode in detail, culminating with a scene of Francis receiving the stigmata, shot laser-like from a six-winged seraph.

THE STORIES of saints are rife with hardship and suffering, the more the better. I can understand this, to a degree. Saints are often misunderstood and rarely accepted in their lifetimes. Challenging the status quo, living a life contrary to society, they are often rejected and lonely. Harder for me are the legends and miracles and the behaviors that are often described as "superhuman," which I find establish distance between saints and ordinary people. Dorothy Day, for example, a prolific writer, thinker, and founder of *The Catholic Worker*, was, in many ways, Franciscan. When it was suggested that she was a saint, she replied, "I won't be dismissed that easily." Sometimes the accounts of saints' lives are so full of difficulty, so miraculous as to strain credulity; these accounts seem to remove the person to another realm of existence altogether. This is ironic, considering that Francis, who humanized God, had every intention of bringing God closer to people.

My struggle with the miracle of the stigmata also relates

to my having lost family members to cancer. I currently know still more individuals who suffer from cancer, as well as Parkinson's disease, or some other debilitating illness. I don't think any of them would have chosen the curtailment of meaningful activities that comes with the suffering.

I wrestled with these thoughts as I approached and stood reverently in the Chapel of the Stigmata, which is considered the most holy place on the mountain. I paused there for some time, but I found no answer to my questions and left, deciding that I didn't need answers and that I was content with mystery and ambiguity.

I later found a greater sense of inspiration and mystery of Francis in the deep cleft of rock below it, the *sasso spicco*. It was the next morning, when Jane and I walked down the steps into this deep crevice. We were temporarily out of the wind—a fierce reminder of Mother Nature, as Francis called her—and sudden silence and stillness added to the drama and beauty. This was the original site that captured Francis: seven meters deep, four meters across, one side juts out as a kind of "roof," and it was in this spot that Francis often came to pray. As I stood underneath the rock, I imagined him 800 years earlier, crouching there with his friars in prayer and silence, no buildings above, just a gigantic cathedral of nature around them containing the simplicity and the beauty of Francis's world. I understood Francis in this simple spot more than any other at La Verna.

This was the impression and essence of La Verna that we would take with us as we departed on the next stage of our journey to Assisi.

Sasso Spicco

7

Pilgrimage as Ritual

Western people are a *ritually starved* people, and in this are different from most of human history.

Richard Rohr, *Falling Upward: A Spirituality for the Second Half of Life*

AFTER EATING A VERY light breakfast and ordering a packed lunch from the café, we set out from La Verna. It was another brisk morning, so on went extra outer layers. We walked across the parking lot at the back of the monastery as the tour buses rolled in. We turned up a jeep track to the top of Monte Calvano, which at 1,250 meters is slightly higher than La Verna. Brother Wind greeted us again as we began the ascent and accompanied us all the way. We were rewarded and delighted by the stunning 270-degree views as we crossed the grassy meadow on the mountaintop. As a mountain biker passed us, he stopped, and we exchanged greetings and took photos for each other.

The views tempted me to pause here longer, but we were eager to keep going. Brother Wind was pushing us, and so we started heading downward (finally!) after days of long ascents. Our destination for the day, Pieve Santo Stefano, was still 13 kilometers away, but we would descend nearly 900 meters to reach it as we entered the upper reaches of the Tiber River Valley.

At the edge of the meadow we went through a gate and then plunged back into the forest along narrow dirt paths. Brother Wind diminished the more we descended, but we could see the havoc he had wrought, evidenced by the number of downed trees on the path that we had to scramble over or under. On each side of the path—especially at the tops of the mountains—was devastation, worse than any we had seen two days before. Limbs were blown down, trees snapped off halfway up their trunks, their tops twisted and caught on one another. At one point we were halted by a downed pine so large and broad that it completely blocked the path. Fortunately, there was a crew clearing downed trees, and just as we were trying to figure out how to get past it, one of the loggers came along with a chainsaw and sliced the trunk in front of us, allowing us to pass. Soon after that we reached our last summit of the day, Monte della Modina, and then welcomed a long downhill trek to our hotel in Pieve Santo Stefano. Somewhere along that part of the journey, the air calmed and our companion, Brother Wind, left us for good.

LEAVING La Verna also meant that we entered the blessed "middle" part of our pilgrimage with a week behind us and ten days ahead. Thoughts and concerns of home faded into the background—our return was too far ahead to think about or plan for it. Now we focused on each day for itself. We were becoming used to the demands of daily walking and climbing and entered a stretch of the route that was less physically challenging, which was a relief. While virtually no stretch of the Way of St. Francis is flat, the elevations for the next week would be considerably easier. We would trace the Upper Tiber Valley through a chain of small, walled cities— Pieve Santo Stefano, Sansepolcro, and Città di Castello— before crossing a lower range of the Apennines to Gubbio.

The first days were sunny and warm. Our biggest challenge was no longer the ascents (which were gentle), but the descents, which could be steep and rocky. Some stretches were monotonous, such as the floodplains below the dam at Lago di Montedoglio, a reservoir of the Tiber; some were perilous, such as the busy highway (with no shoulder) entering Sansepolcro. We endured minor hip pain and two days of stormy weather, which forced us to take a bus rather than risk the higher rocky trails.[1]

Meeting up with other pilgrims outside Pietralunga

The gifts of this stretch were quite simply time itself and the awareness that we had all of it that we wanted and had no particular demands on us. I reflected as I walked that this was why I went on pilgrimage and what I had been missing for the two previous years while we waited out the pandemic, mostly at home.

Ever since 2018, when I had the chance to walk the Camino to Santiago de Compostela, I have become increasingly enthusiastic about the ancient spiritual/religious ritual of pilgrimage. With its intentionality and its particular spiritual goals, pilgrimage is different from tourism. It was a common practice in the Middle Ages in

Europe, when it meant either walking to a local or regional shrine or taking a more arduous (and often dangerous) trek to a distant site, such as Jerusalem, Rome, or Santiago.

Pilgrimage routes and practices likely existed during prehistory. Places such as Stonehenge or Avebury in England, or Newgrange in Ireland, existed in the midst of vast sacred landscapes filled with multiple burial tombs, stone circles for tracking the solar and lunar cycles, and lined avenues used for ritual processions. The precise meaning of these has been lost to history, but their dominance over the landscape and their use over thousands of years suggest that they were destinations for pilgrimage.[2]

Ancient pilgrimage routes still exist around the world and are part of all major religious traditions. For example, one of the Five Pillars of Islam is that a Muslim man ought (at least once in his life) to make the Hajj (pilgrimage) to Mecca. Japanese Buddhists have the 1,200-year-old Shikoku Pilgrimage, an 1,150-kilometer circuit of 88 Buddhist shrines. (The latter's antiquity coincides with pilgrimage to Santiago de Compostela, which also began about 1,200 years ago.)

The modern resurgence of pilgrimage is due, in part, to a deeper spiritual search that goes beyond what is offered through common religious institutions and practices. In Europe, it has been aided by an initiative from the Council of Europe, which created a series of Cultural Routes, the first of which was the Camino Frances, the most popular route to Santiago de Compostela, designated in 1987.[3]

One of my favorite authors, Robert Macfarlane, who searched for and walked many of the ancient tracks around the world, has written of the modern, inner urge to go on pilgrimage:

It represents a return of imperfectly deleted religion. And it is surely part of a broader desire to reconnect with landscape and nature, provoked by the increasing dematerialization and disembodiment of virtualized existence. While we find it easy to say what we make of places, we are far less good at saying what places make of us—and as Rowan Williams puts it: "Place works on the pilgrim . . . that's what pilgrimage is for."[4]

In an effort to recover this ancient practice, Jane and I have devoted much of the past five years—as much as the pandemic allowed us to travel—to recovering the ritual of pilgrimage on foot or bicycle for ourselves. It's becoming a new "vocation" or "calling" for me, through both writing about and hosting hiking and pilgrimage tours. We "connect with landscape and nature," often for five or six hours at a time, continually outdoors, which has its own effects. The landscape we crossed in Italy was an old landscape, even a sacred landscape. And, as Rowan Williams wrote, that place "worked" itself upon us.

In walking—particularly on pilgrimage—all the rhythms of my life get reset. Walking forces me to go slowly—forces me to use time, not to measure it. Too often our lives are gauged in relation to what we are planning to do, what we are not able to do, what we wish we could do, rather than what we are currently doing. When we walk on pilgrimage, we may seem to accomplish very little; the possibilities and demands upon us narrow. I am aware that I could have gone from one place to another much faster via car, train, or bus, but at what cost? I go on pilgrimage to force myself to walk, to move my interior life into another state, one in which time is not a premium, but rather something that comes *to* me, renewed, every day, not unlike manna.[5] On a pilgrimage, as these rhythms reset, I am able to let the trail and the pilgrimage unfold ahead of me, receiving what comes along, instead of planning and calculating what will come next. Time is not a commodity to be spent or rationed, but one to be simply enjoyed and experienced. After we had been on this journey for a week, Jane and I no longer felt in a hurry. There was nothing to do but walk, at our own pace, to our next destination and look out for the unexpected along the way, such as pilgrims we might meet and share a meal with, ancient churches with amazing frescoes, or hosts who would take us on a tour of their town.

War memorial for "all the victims of war" in Sansepolcro

During the two years that interrupted this pilgrimage, I observed how the pandemic took us all in directions that we may not have chosen. In the United States, it started something called the Great Resignation, in which millions of people, representing a broad demographic, simply left what they were doing, their work in particular. All of the reasons are not known. Was it a reflection on mortality? A chance to pause and refocus life? An awareness of the meaninglessness of some jobs or of modern life and economies? For me it had a paradoxically opposite effect: since I couldn't travel, I took a full-time job teaching older adults online. Isolation hit the older adult population especially hard, so I had huge classes for the first year. Ironically, it was about "slow" travel —such as pilgrimage—that I taught about the most, and what my learners wanted to hear about the most.

I noticed, unfortunately, that it also created a turbo-charged dependence upon digital technology, resulting in a yearning to find "real" and "embodied," practices, to have face-to-face relationships once again. We wanted in-person, "actual" versus "virtual" experiences. I reflected, as we walked, that one of the curious things about my job was that while it was supposedly about helping people feel less lonely, it made me feel more lonely. When businesses and travel reopened in the fall of 2021, I was stuck at home, having to teach and prepare for a full schedule of classes—making me feel lonelier than ever. So, when the new year arrived and Italy reopened for travel, I realized that I needed to make a change. I gave notice at my job, and Jane and I prepared to return to Italy for three weeks. I needed to return to my "vocation" of walking and writing about it.

Each day was now rich with the rituals of pilgrimage: discovery, surprise, history, culture, and cuisine, and our spirits reveled in it. And, along the highway between Sansepolcro and Citta di Castello, on our way to Gubbio, we crossed over from Tuscany to Umbria, Francis's homeland.

8

Stones and Wolves

An indication of the tenacity of St. Francis' grip on men's hearts lies in the frequency with which his life story—fact and legend intertwined—has been told and retold... the powerful memories of the sweetness of his character would not die...

Sarel Eimerl, *The World of Giotto*

A PILGRIM MIGHT WALK weeks to experience a day as beautiful as the one on which we walked to Gubbio: sunshine after a day of rain, fresh green hillsides, colorful wildflowers, soft warm air. It was a reminder that the real pilgrim's destination is the path itself—the time, the beauty, the challenges, the vistas, and an unhurried pace.

The day before, we had walked 15 kilometers from the small mountain town of Pietralunga under a dark gray sky and through occasional downpours. The road had been a mixture of asphalt and dirt, but the rain had turned some of

that dirt into very deep mud, making for slippery and occasionally dangerous footing. Our final descent had been into
Loretto, a small settlement standing at the upper end of a
river valley about 10 kilometers from Gubbio. One last
downpour commenced just before we found our small
cottage at B&B Di Valle on the outskirts of the village. We
phoned our host, who we knew was away for the weekend.
She didn't speak English, and we struggled to understand
where to find the key she had left for us, finally figuring out
that it was under a mat on the porch. We were drenched by
the time we unlocked the door. Thankfully, the cottage was
modern and well fitted, dry, and warm. We enjoyed a long,
hot shower, a comfortable bed, and the snacks that were laid
out for us.

Entering Umbria, we were now in the heart of Francis's
homeland, the places that he frequented, the people that he
knew best. The people there loved him then, and they still
do today.

PULLING on our packs the next morning, we stepped out
into the gorgeous day and were treated immediately to the
sweet fragrance of wisteria. The garden fences outside the
cottage were draped in it, with droplets from the previous
day's rain slowly falling from the flowerets.

The clouds and rain had masked our view of the valley
the day before, but now all was fresh and green and inviting.
Large clouds raced overhead, casting shadows that climbed
up the patchwork of olive groves and pastures on the slopes
of the valley. Above the clouds, a blue sky peeked through
with the promise of a dry and sunny day.

Just 200 meters down the road from where we had
stayed was San Giovanni Bautista, the ancient church of

Loretto. A humble stone structure, there was nothing about it that distinguished it from any of the other village churches we had passed along the way, but we decided to see if it was open. No historical marker stood outside; there was no particular artistic or architectural element that drew us. We approached the wooden door and gave the latch a try. Often, these churches are locked, but not this one. The latch lifted, and I gently pushed open the door, stepped in, and slipped off my pack. We had discovered a treasure.

I looked at an information sheet (in Italian) tacked to the inside of the door. Using my phone to translate, I read that the church had been rebuilt in 1236 upon an earlier church of the 11th century. The history described was eloquent:

> Says a writer of the time, Rodolfo Glabro, that in the first century after the year 1,000 . . . with the rebirth of human activity, it seemed that the world had shaken and, freeing itself from her old age, dressed herself in a white mantle of churches.
>
> In the Gubbio territory the churches built in the eleventh century were modest, rectangular buildings, often covered with a barrel vault, in that Romanesque style, stripped of ornaments and bas-reliefs. Yet they expressed an austere religiosity that looked at the essential, which grant nothing to feeling, but everything to adoration.
>
> These churches, built along the dusty streets or on the edge of the woods, were for all the place of prayer and peace; poor knelt on the bare floor as well as the rich; servants and feudal lords felt like brothers. These churches were the expression of the religiosity of our people and many of them were built by the Benedictine monks of our nearby monasteries.

I took note of the 1236 date: just a decade after the death of Francis. The statement "servants and feudal lords felt like brothers" had a distinctly Franciscan feel. I read further that beneath the altar was the crypt of the original, still more ancient church.

As I finished reading about the history of the church, I was greeted by a gray-bearded, spry man with a knitted cap, a large backpack, and a huge smile. Had I not known better, I might've thought one of the medieval monks had appeared to give me a tour of the church. "Luigi is my name," he said, introducing himself, "but I'm Aloysius at home in Austria." We didn't know it, but we had just come across a very experienced pilgrim. His English was excellent, and he asked if he could accompany us inside the church.

The interior was dimly lit, but we could see its beautiful stone-vaulted ceiling, a rarity for a country church, which more typically had wooden rafters. A single half-circle window above the apse lit the interior. I paused to let my eyes adjust to the faint light, sensing with awe the old stones.

We descended into the crypt, itself lit by a single window at one end, but with electric lights tucked up inside the arched vaults. A single, small slab-marble altar sat at one end.

It is important not to rush into or out of these places, but to take the time to contemplate and think of the tens of thousands who may have entered and offered a prayer over the centuries. Places like this, humble and holy, full of the depth and breadth of human history, perhaps not listed in the tour books—these are the places that I go on pilgrimage to discover.

I paused and touched the stone walls, something I do in ancient structures. I think of the hands that had quarried and dressed the stones, hauled them to the site, and then laid them in place. Did the masons envision the final structure as they worked? Did they wonder how long it would last? To me such stones represented the conjunction of the natural world (stone) and human vision and effort (the architect and the stonemason), a new creation in which humans become involved in the evolution of the world itself, creating something new and awe-inspiring out of the very building blocks of the earth.

The crypt of the church

I recalled how Francis—who might have helped build the stone walls of Assisi in his youth—had reconstructed old churches. He had begged for stones, cherishing and blessing each that he was given. We stood in silence a few more moments before we ascended the steps and headed out the door.

Luigi accompanied us toward Gubbio for the next hour, telling us of his adventures. Well into his seventies, he had gone on a pilgrimage somewhere in the world every year for the past two decades, typically in Europe. He told us he was on his way to Assisi for "at least the tenth time" and offered, "Pilgrimage expands my understanding of the world." I paused after I heard those words.

"That," I said, "is the best definition I've ever heard of pilgrimage."

The ever-widening valley grew more gorgeous with every step: olive groves, vineyards, grazing cattle, and sheep. Brilliant green grew up to the tops of the low ridges. Gubbio, spread upward on the slopes of Mount Ingino, gradually came into view. We passed through several small settlements, greeting with a hearty *"Buongiorno!"* people who were out working their gardens on this spectacular morning. We always received a wave, a smile, and a greeting in return.

We parted with Luigi as we neared a village; he wanted a café and some refreshment, we were eager to get into Gubbio, now only a few kilometers away. We said farewell, but we would see him again.

GUBBIO IS AN ANCIENT TOWN. The hills above it were first settled in the Bronze Age over 3,000 years ago by the Umbrians, an Italic tribe that preceded both the Romans and the Etruscans. It later became an important Roman settlement (Iguvium) before the first century B.C.E. On its outskirts are well-preserved ruins of the Roman amphitheater that could seat 6,000 people, one of the largest in the Roman empire. The old city walls are still visible on the mountainside, gradually leading up to the Palazzo Ducale and then continuing to its *duomo* (cathedral), San Giacomo. Farther up, crowning the mountain, is a church dedicated to Saint Ubaldo.

Strolling through Gubbio's medieval quarter we could feel Francis's presence, and it was here, strangely, not La Verna, where I felt it more. Here in Gubbio, which honors one of the most famous Franciscan legends, I felt him among the people. There was so much to see here that we decided to stay an extra day.

We climbed halfway through the town to reach our lodging in a monastery, the Instituto Maestre Pie Filippini, and pressed the entry buzzer. A short, older nun, dressed in a modest habit, greeted us. She spoke no English. We said our names, and she gave a look of recognition and motioned for us to follow her inside. We passed through a central hall, then found an elevator that took us to the next floor. We followed her through a labyrinth of hallways until we came to the guest lounge and kitchen. She pointed to the refrigerator and then showed us to our room, all the while instructing us (in Italian) about the house rules. She paused to look at us, lifted her head, and widened her eyes as if we were to respond. We needed to tell her that we didn't speak Italian and asked if she spoke English. "*Non parliamo italiano. In inglese, per favore?*" but this was futile. This was our first stay in an "religious house," and it turned out that except for us and the two nuns, we were alone in this *huge* place.

Medieval Quarter of Gubbio

Gubbio shares two significant events in the life of Francis. Only about 50 kilometers from Assisi, this is country that he frequented. The first recorded appearance of the city in his life was in 1205, shortly after he left Assisi in his self-imposed exile—when he had "disowned" his family. He set out for Gubbio, along an ancient road we would soon follow, to an old friend from his boyhood, Giacomello Spadalunga, also the wealthy son of a cloth merchant.

He had not gotten far on that journey before he ran into trouble. Wearing little more than rags, singing in French like a troubadour, he was beaten and tossed in a ditch outside

Valfabbrica, by a band of robbers who thought him mad, though they were more likely disappointed that he had no money. Bruised and cold, he sought refuge in a nearby Benedictine monastery, but they also thought him mad and fed him only some scraps before sending him on his way. He arrived in Gubbio at his friend Giacomello's home, hungry, nearly naked, and penniless.

We don't know the exact origin of the friendship between Giacomello and Francis—they may have been imprisoned together in Perugia after that failed battle. But he welcomed Francis warmly, giving him food and lodging and new clothing—a hermit's garb, consisting of a tunic and belt along with sandals and a staff. The tradition of hospitality and charity that began on that first visit must have been profound, because eventually the Spadalunga warehouse became a monastery. Next to it arose the spacious Basilica di San Francesco, a beautiful structure with a statue of Francis and a wolf out in front.

THERE ARE a multitude of stories about Francis's interactions with animals of all kinds—ducks, rabbits, hogs, mice, fish, and especially flocks of birds. As with any of the legends of his life, it is not easy to separate fact from fiction, but the legend of how he tamed the wolf that terrorized Gubbio may perhaps be the best known, and it is my favorite. *The Little Flowers of Saint Francis,* a highly embellished 14th-century collection of these legends about Francis, tells it like this:

> In the days when St. Francis abode in the city of Gubbio, a huge wolf, terrible and fierce, appeared in the neighborhood, and not only devoured animals but men also; in

such wise that all citizens went in great fear of their lives, because ofttimes the wolf came close to the city. And when they went abroad, all men armed themselves as they were going forth to battle; and even so none who chanced on the wolf alone could defend himself; and at last it came to such a pass that for fear of this wolf no man durst leave the city walls.[1]

Francis, out of compassion for the people of the city, found and then confronted the wolf. According to *Little Flowers* the wolf, teeth bared, "leapt toward Francis" but was stopped by Francis giving the sign of the cross. Addressing him as "Brother Wolf," Francis admonished the animal for having attacked and killed "both men and cattle" and for terrorizing the people. But then, rather than condemning him, he extracted from the creature a promise to change his ways and become peaceful. Francis, in turn, vowed that he would obtain a promise from the people that they would not try to take revenge for what the wolf had done. The wolf responded obediently, bowed his head, and "lifted his right paw and gently laid it in the hand of Francis, giving him thereby such token of good faith as he could." Immediately afterward, the wolf "set forth his side even as a pet lamb," as they walked side-by-side into the central square. In front of the marveling townspeople, Francis again obtained the promise from the wolf, who signified his acceptance in front of the town by bowing his head, wagging his tail, and offering his paw for a shake.

Thereafter, according to the legend, "Brother Wolf" no longer terrorized the townspeople but went peacefully from home to home where they fed him. He lived two more years before dying.

The legend fascinates me because of the way Francis

played the "just" peacemaker, extracting a promise from the people of Gubbio to feed the wolf. This acknowledged that the wolf's behavior was due, in part, to his natural instinct to hunt for his food. In other words, the wolf also had needs, which Francis understood; this is why he didn't condemn him to death, or miraculously drive him away, as others might have done. Francis achieved not only a truce but *reconciliation* as an alternative to retribution.

As with any legend of Francis, its historicity is open to doubt. The story might be a conflation of several legends circulating at the time of Francis taming wolves in the mountain villages. Some historians speculate that the wolf may have been an outlawed lord of the countryside who terrorized the people. Whatever the source or origin—wolf or lord—the Franciscan historian André Vauchez, points to an even deeper significance in the story, concerning the roots of violence:

Francis resolved the conflict by negotiating the wolf's right to reside in the town and, probably, to receive financial reimbursement since according to the legend the wolf was maintained to the end of his life at the expense of the commune. But whichever reading [wolf or lord] we give to this account its lesson is the same: between the human person and the animal, as in relationship between human beings, exclusion is at the origin of violence, whereas a fraternal and welcoming attitude makes its object aware of the joy of being included and prompts that individual to make peace.[2]

FRANCIS, who had made service and care for lepers—the outcasts of society—a priority of his ministry, would have understood what it meant for any being to be an outcast. That gives the story, if not credibility, at least a deeper and lasting meaning.

The story of the wolf came to life as we walked around Gubbio. The old city walls are still intact, the wooded mountainside above them extremely steep, and I can imagine how they might have once felt dangerous. Near the top of the city, just below the old walls, we came to the tiny Chiesa di San Francesco della Pace, reconstructed in the 16th century over the purported cave of the wolf. Inside the crypt below we came across a medieval sarcophagus lid found nearby in 1873.

I read that the stone covered the bones of an animal—a veterinarian confirmed that they were the remains of a wolf.

The stone sarcophagus of the wolf

9

The Ambience of History

It seemed to me that the remembrance of human activities at certain locations vested them with a kind of sacredness that could not have been obtained otherwise.

Vine Deloria, *God Is Red*

ON OUR FIRST night in Gubbio we took a cable car from the city up to the church dedicated to Saint Ubaldo, near the top of Mount Ingino. Looking south over the valley and the low mountains, we made out the silhouette of Mount Subasio as it bulged out from the Apennines 30 kilometers distant. Assisi, our goal, lay on a spur of that mountain. The old pathway there was longer—it twisted and turned for 50 kilometers—so it would take us three days to walk it. Seeing our final destination filled us with a mixture of excitement and anticipation, but also a bit of sadness since it would be the end of our pilgrimage.

Between Mounts Ingino and Subasio, and Gubbio and Assisi, lies a sacred terrain that Francis frequented. It is a land of remembrance and legends about him—many of them true—as well as a land of great beauty; he would have passed through it on his way to Gubbio and then to La Verna. In recent decades the track from Gubbio to Assisi was also one of the first marked paths of the Way of St. Francis, appropriately named the "Peace Walk," and like the entire Way of St. Francis, it connects significant sights in his life.

We left Gubbio on a straight road that headed due south, up into what were more like foothills than mountains. Once up into them, the path followed the contours of the land, sweeping around the steeper hills, curving in and out of the folds of the ravines, descending into and then climbing out from frequent stream crossings. This felt like a different landscape than what we had encountered in the higher mountains—tamer, more cultivated. And we did not feel enclosed as we had in the forest—the views were open and wide. We could easily imagine Francis and his friars walking these same pathways in the springtime, just like us. It was an inhabited countryside in his time, as it is now, with castles on the hill-tops, and it is dotted with monasteries, small villages, farm-steads, churches, and, more recently, modern agriturismo and villas. Woven among those was a beautiful tapestry of groomed pastures, quilted with stands of hardwoods and the occasional vineyard and olive grove.

Looking back to Gubbio

Gubbio stayed in view behind us for the first three hours as we slowly climbed on asphalt and smooth gravel roads and forded two streams. We knew that there would be no place to buy food along the way this day, so we had stocked up on at a large *supermercato* on the edge of Gubbio. The sky was gray, pierced with holes of blue, and the weather dry. We were leaving Gubbio under the same racing clouds that had brought us there. We were so used to climbing that by now the 500 meters we ascended that day seemed easy. We breathed in the subtle perfume of the wildflowers: The pastures and fields of the Umbrian countryside were bursting with red poppies, yellow buttercups, and dande-lions. The paths in the neatly pruned vineyards were mowed, and the air smelled of freshly cut grass. Fruit trees were in bloom, and the tree leaves were emerging out of the bud, some already in full leaf.

∼

WALKING through this sacred and rich historical landscape brought to mind James Herriot's recollection of Yorkshire: "[T]he first thing that enthralled me about Yorkshire was its wild beauty, the feeling of remoteness and solitude that keeps one's sense of wonder alive; but as time went on I realized there was something else: the strong ambience of history. The distant past seemed somehow close at hand."[1]

It is walking through a landscape of history, habitation, and cultivation that makes European trekking different from backpacking at home. People ask us why we go to Italy (or Spain or anywhere in Europe) to hike, and why we don't just do this near home. After all, the Appalachian Trail (AT) in the Eastern United States is 3,500 kilometers long and just a 45-minute drive from our home. Why not just hike there?

This is a good question, partly answered by saying that we do go on day hikes on the AT near home. We love being outside, and we love the beauty of the Blue Ridge Mountains. But it's not the same. What's missing is the ambience of history, the connections of landscape, history, and culture to the sacred. While there was—and still is—sacredness in the land of the United States for the indigenous peoples who lived closely with the land, that sacredness was not appreciated by many of those who emigrated from Europe and had different spiritual traditions. The history of Europeans in the United States is not deep, only four hundred years at the most. My own ancestors moved around too much, and we didn't and still don't have that deep connection with the land, which is one reason we are so apt to exploit and spoil it. We are poorer for that loss of connection, and that is one reason I am drawn to these places in Europe where that history and connection run deep. The mountains near me are beautiful, and I, at least, consider them sacred. But without the connection to a deep past, it's just not the same as it feels in Europe.

~

PART OF THAT "AMBIENCE OF HISTORY" was our destination for that night: the Eremo di San Pietro in Vigneto (Hermitage of St. Peter's in the Vineyard) 16 kilometers away. Once a Benedictine monastery and pilgrim hostel, the church was already in existence in the 13th century. It would have been familiar to Francis, and he very likely stopped there.

We arrived at the *eremo* in midafternoon after taking a leisurely pace. We were warmly welcomed by Primo and Nadia, volunteers who ran the place, along with Antonio, the gardener. It is a pilgrims-only hostel, one of a handful that exist right now along the Way of St. Francis. And there is no charge—it's run on donations only. Pilgrims join in communal meals and stay in a 14-bed dormitory. We were the only ones there that night. The fact that it is run on donations and by volunteers give it an authentic pilgrim atmosphere. In medieval times, pilgrims were typically hosted at pilgrim hostels—"hospitals" as they were known then— run by religious orders whose vocation was to look after pilgrims. The Eremo di San Pietro is run by the Italian Confraternity of St. James in Perugia, a group of Italians who support the Camino de Santiago. Besides this location, they run an *albergue* or pilgrim hostel (San Nicolas) along the Camino Frances and another one in Rome.

Eremo San Pietro in Vigneto

We were told shortly after arriving that supper was at 7:00, and that there would be a foot washing service and pilgrim blessing in the chapel at 6:30—but only if we wanted it, which we said we did. We took showers, napped, and then walked around the peaceful and beautiful grounds of the monastery, which still include several hermitages, used now for private retreats. I admired the beautiful stonework of the buildings, which had to be over 800 years old. They exuded the deep history of its past as a place of pilgrim hospitality, of a place of prayer and contemplation, of rest for the spirit. We ended our walk in the restored chapel, walls painted blue, with 15th-century frescoes above the altar.

The foot washing service was largely symbolic. A small blessing was read by Primo (for me) and by Nadia (for Jane) before a handful of water was poured over our feet. They read it in Italian, but I translated it later for them:

> We heartily welcome you to our place of hospitality on behalf of the Confraternity of St. James of Italy, from which our clothing bears the scallop shell.
>
> According to an ancient tradition we welcome pilgrims with the washing of feet. This simple gesture is rich in tradition—Jesus washed the feet of his friends and taught them to do the same. Repeating it this evening means that we freely welcome you, as He taught us, in a spirit of service and friendship.
>
> This moment reminds us that Jesus himself is present in a pilgrimage and anyone who walks it, walks it in the spirit of Christ, and he or she who walks it, walks in Christ.
>
> [Ritual of water poured over feet]
>
> In the spirit of Christ, we welcome you to our place of hospitality, to San Pietro in Vigneto. May rest comfort you and give you the strength to continue to Assisi, Rome, La Verna.

Our adopted faith is Mennonite, and foot washing on Maundy Thursday is one of our treasured traditions, so we appreciated this ritual and blessing.

Afterward, we were treated to supper, which was followed by an amazing evening of conversation—amazing because Primo, Nadia, and Antonio spoke little English and we even less Italian. In spite of that they discovered that I had walked the Camino Frances four years before and then shared how the three of them had walked it and how it had changed their lives. We have discovered over the years that people can meet at a soul level, despite language barriers. The beauty of the place, the inner connection, the service to pilgrims—this was the perfect experience as we neared our destination. We left the next morning after breakfast with lunches packed. Our three hosts had gathered to give us a pilgrim blessing as we departed, a wonderful start to our penultimate day on the path.

Primo, Nadia and Antonio gather to give us a farewell blessing

THE WALK to Valfabbrica was under a blue sky. The path followed closely the contours of the foothills as they wound above the river Chiascio, which is now dammed to create a reservoir, and both were in our sight the entire day. There were more descents to stream crossings than the day before —I counted seven—and fortunately we made our way across with dry feet each time. The previous week's rain had soaked the ground, however, and there was a lot of deep mud, which made progress slow, but the gorgeous scenery and the fresh spring air made up for it. We passed pilgrims going both ways—from Austria, Italy, and the Netherlands —the most we had seen in any single day so far. They seemed amazed that two Americans knew about this path, and they were also amazed—incredulous, actually—that we were walking it in hiking sandals instead of the heavier hiking boots that so many Europeans favor. They asked and we explained that they were actually the most comfortable thing for hiking, especially for someone like me with flat feet.

There was more "ambience of history," as we passed the tiny stone church of Caprignone, where Francis had attended a meeting of the first Franciscan friars in 1223. The friars had rebuilt the church atop an earlier, ruined one that had been constructed atop a pagan temple. The building was locked, but it reminded us that this was Francis's path.

We passed the castle of Biscina—one of three bastions that we would pass or see that day—and it served as a reminder of Italy's violent history. In his book about the painter Giotto, Sarel Eimerl wrote, "Never noted for its calm, Italy in the 13th century was one vast hubbub of battle. Popes and emperors warred for sovereignty, princes for realms, cities for trading advantage. Almost every locality had its views and alignments: clan versus clan, noble versus commoner, upper versus lower bourgeois, the laboring poor versus them all. Seething enmities awaited only a spark to erupt. . . . Yet along with the strife there was striving; with the violence vigor; and with the bloodthirstiness a taste for beauty."[2]

The castle, which existed in some form in Francis's time, had seen better days, though it looked imposing from a distance. Someone had started to renovate it, but now it looked abandoned. Its tumble-down appearance, along with the warning tape along the entrances, prevented us from exploring it more.

The frequent climbs and descents wore us out by early afternoon. We came to a junction where we could choose a more "scenic" path that would reward us with great vistas and more ancient churches and castles, or an easier, though more monotonous, route along a blacktopped road that would shave off distance, time, and—most of all—climbing. The choice at that point was easy, and we opted to take the easier route, which got us to our destination earlier and with enough time to get in a good nap before supper.

OUR LAST DAY to Assisi was superb: blue sky, warm temperatures, soft breezes, and green everywhere—the air smelled of spring. We had stayed the night before in Valfabbrica in guestrooms of Sui Passi di Francesco, which literally means "in the steps of Francis." The balcony off of our room looked across the road toward the old medieval quarter of the town, the tower of the castle on top still keeping silent watch. Passing below its walls, we set off on a blacktop road to the edge of town, where we picked up a dirt road through a forest—a path called *Fosso de Lupe* (Ditch of the Wolves)—a reminder of its wild past.

The old town walls of Valfabbrica

This path was the muddiest yet, and we picked our way around large puddles and stepped gently through small stream crossings. We came to a long, steep ascent along this pathway where the water had cut a ditch so deep that we had to straddle it awkwardly as we climbed, finally coming to steps carved into the dirt on one side that made the going a bit easier. We passed a group of pilgrims from Austria who we had met the night before at supper—the same group that had asked about our sandals.

We walked this way for nearly an hour before the path broadened out to a gravel road alongside brilliant fields of red poppies, yellow dandelions, and white Queen Anne's lace. Soon we were at the top of a ridge, and at a juncture of the road we came to the church and cemetery of San Nicolò. I wanted to explore it and was disappointed that the gate was chained. But my disappointment didn't last long, because when we turned to our right and looked ahead, we saw our first glimpse of Assisi, just seven kilometers ahead: the Basilica of San Francesco sitting unmistakably on the edge of town, with the Rocca Maggiore, a medieval castle, to its left, high on the mountain above.

The end of our pilgrimage was again in sight.

The Basilica of Saint Francis in the distance

PART II

Rome to Rieti, September 2022

Distance: 105 kilometers
2700 meters elevation

10

The Opposite Direction

To return to the source, one must travel in the opposite direction.

René Daumal, *Mount Analogue*

The pilgrim is a poetic traveler, one who believes that there is poetry on the road, at the heart of everything.

Phil Cousineau, *The Art of Pilgrimage*

I STOOD in the noonday sun in St. Peter's Square in the Vatican in Rome, one of the world's great pilgrim destinations, a place that millions travel *to* each year. The iconic dome of the basilica dominated the wide, tourist-filled plaza. Like the crowds, I had arrived, but this was not my final destination—it was my point of departure. From here I was *leaving*, going in the opposite direction, *away* from Rome, toward Assisi. I was heading north along the Way of St.

Francis, hoping to arrive in Rieti in five or six days, a distance of 105 kilometers (about 65 miles).

This was my third journey on the Way of St. Francis, and I was alone this time: no Jane with me. She is a doula, or birth coach, and her work was keeping her busy, with three births to attend. While I always preferred walking with her, she blessed me to go on this journey alone. With that encouragement I would complete the route, returning to our original departure point in Rieti, three years earlier.

I had another purpose in this journey: gathering the spiritual energy and inspiration to continue my work of writing. Pilgrimage has not only ignited my spirit but also kindled my creativity as a writer. While I need this kind of walk to keep myself going physically, the inward conditioning was just as important to me.

JUST MINUTES BEFORE, I had stepped off a train that had brought me from the Rome airport and my red-eye flight from Washington D.C. Sensible people might have headed to a hotel room and a welcome bed. I was, instead, starting my pilgrimage that very day. I had discovered years before that walking in the sunlight is a good way to reset the circadian rhythm, and since the first stage of the Way of St. Francis north out of Rome is only about 15 kilometers, I calculated that, with enough espresso, I could do it.

Departing the station, my tired eyes blinked in the glaring sun and I fished around in my pack for my sunglasses. With them on, I looked above the surrounding buildings and confirmed my starting point: the Dome of St. Peter's. A hot, dusty wind swirled trash around my feet as I stepped in my sandals across a vacant, weedy lot. The streets were oddly empty and quiet: Maybe the locals were home for the *riposo* (siesta), or maybe it was just too hot for the tourists? I should have been fatigued from jet lag, but instead I was energized with a combination of excitement and caffeine and sugar from the cappuccino and croissants that I had consumed at an airport café an hour earlier.

Keeping the Dome in view, I headed north about a hundred meters and then saw the wall. I had been here before and now remembered: The Vatican is a country-within-a-country, surrounded by a wall, situated over a mile from the center of old Rome. To get to St. Peter's I first had to find my way into this tiny country

I finally found a gate and saw cars entering, but a policeman stopped me before I could enter. *"Non, non."* No pedestrians. Not exactly the warmest welcome. He pointed me eastward where I would eventually find a gate that allowed pedestrians. I turned and plodded down a wide sidewalk lined with stalls. They were packed with souvenirs: postcards, rosaries, and various religious trinkets. Photos of the Pope were everywhere. Hawkers called out, and beggars jingled their cups at me as I passed. The street was loud with traffic, horns honking. Diesel fumes mixed with the dust in the hot breeze.

In another five minutes I had reached bustling St. Peter's Square and stood inside its recognizable semicircle of columns. Across from me, snaking lines of tourists waited to get into the Sistine Chapel or Vatican museums. Here were the crowds I was imagining. Rising above us all was the Dome.

I was ready to begin my pilgrimage.

I HEADED toward the pilgrim's office (called the *Opera Romana Pellegrinaggi* or "Roman Agency for Pilgrims") to get a stamp, or *timbro* on my *credenziale*. The office is just off the square, and there was no line inside. I approached the counter and slid my credenziale toward a woman behind a glass screen, asking her to please stamp it. *"Timbro, per favore?"* She smiled and pulled out her rubber stamp, inked it, but paused. She had thought I was completing a pilgrimage to Rome, but my *credenziale* was empty. I pointed toward the first block and said "Assisi" (while pointing north), and then she gave me a nod of comprehension and my first timbro. *"Grazie,"* I said as I turned and exited.

Saint Peter's Square

Rome has been a pilgrimage destination for nearly two millennia, the tombs of its martyrs drawing the faithful from all corners of the globe. Two of the first Apostles, Peter and Paul, were executed there in the first century. As the capital of the Roman Empire, its bishop (there have subsequently been more than 260) became, in time, the head of the Roman Catholic Church, the Pope. Along with Santiago de Compostela and Jerusalem, Rome was one of the three great pilgrimage destinations of the Middle Ages. Well-known and ancient footpaths still lead to it. Since 1929 the Vatican, known as the smallest country in the world both in population and geographic size, has been a sovereign nation. This fact is somewhat strange to me, since I imagine that Jesus never meant the Church to be a sovereign political entity. Still, millions come here each year, many on pilgrimage, but even more as sightseers. St. Peter's Basilica, along with its famed Sistine Chapel and the Vatican Museums, are among the top tourist destinations in Rome.[1]

This place is also home to another Francis, the current Pope as of this writing.[2] This is ironic, since the first Francis is one who never became Pope, never wanted power, never wanted to live in a palace. It's this first Francis I'm looking for, and I'm setting out again to find him by walking through the Italian landscape. I was intending to journey northward, away from this legendary place, away from the crowds, my path eventually leading outside the city and into the countryside.

NO SIGNPOST INDICATED where I was to begin. I looked around beautiful St. Peter's Square, saw two tourists attempting a selfie, and offered to help them. They agreed and handed me their phone, and I took several photos of them. They in turn took some of me with the Dome of St. Peter's in the background. They spoke English and told me they were from Poland. They asked where I was from, and I told them Virginia in the United States. I added that I was walking toward Assisi. They gave me an enthusiastic and understanding nod and uttered a blessing to me for my journey. I received that blessing as a "sign" that I was officially launching my pilgrimage.

I looked around the square and noted a bronze sculpture called "Angels Unaware," dedicated to the world's (and history's) refugees and migrants. The monument is striking: It shows 140 life-size figures, contemporary and historical, of all cultures, young and old—Africans, European Jews, Syrians, among them—shoulder to shoulder on a crowded boat. I had first seen it in 2019 right after it was dedicated, and I found it a moving memorial, in particular because it is in the Vatican's central square. I approached and took a photo of my hand upon it, thinking it an apt departure point for a pilgrim.

Angels Unaware by Canadian sculptor Timothy P. Schmalz.

With that gesture, I was off. But I got barely 100 meters before realizing how thirsty I was in the heat, which was over 30 degrees Celsius (about 85 degrees Fahrenheit). On the crowded sidewalk heading eastward, alongside the stalls of saints' medals, and postcards of St. Peter's Basilica, I spied a man selling bottles of ice-cold water. I bought one. I downed it quickly and bought another, rubbing the icy bottle on my hot forehead. In this pause a young man from Sierra Leone, dressed all in white, and with impeccable English, approached me. He asked if I was a pilgrim, and I said that I was, bound for Assisi. He smiled and suddenly clapped a bracelet around my wrist, tightening it as he announced another blessing upon me. The bracelet was made of brown leather and an oval medallion with an elephant. No doubt he sold these to tourists in this square. I offered to pay, but he shook his head. "No, for pilgrims it is free." I accepted this additional blessing on my journey, thanked him, and exited the Vatican eastward, down the Via Della Conciliazione toward the Tiber River.

The Way of St. Francis has no route markings at this stage; it requires a guidebook or GPX tracks on a mobile phone to navigate. But for me, at this point, it was simply about getting out of Rome. My goal that day was Monte Sacro, in the northern part of the city, through 15 kilometers of urban walking. I was thinking it would take me about three hours. But first I needed to find a shop where I could reload a data plan for the Italian SIM card on my phone. I had hoped to find a shop in the airport but hadn't. I knew that TIM, the mobile phone carrier I was looking for, was quite common, and I was sure I would come across a shop. The woman in the pilgrim office told me that I would find one on an adjacent street radiating out from the square, but first I wanted to walk around the Castel Sant'Angelo and catch a glimpse of the Tiber River.

The Castel was originally built in the second century as a monumental tomb for Emperor Hadrian, but over the next thousand years it was transformed into a defensive structure. Eventually it became the Pope's fortress. It is an imposing structure: tall, round, surrounded on all sides by a star-shaped moat. Crowds lounged and posed for selfies by the river; a guy with an electric guitar played "Stairway to Heaven," a tune I found ironic in that setting. I headed along the river and bought a sandwich and an apple in a small grocery and another bottle of ice-cold water. I crossed a bridge and turned northeast, into the thick of the city.

The classic Roman Umbrella Pine

For the next two hours I made slow progress on my frustrating journey to find a TIM shop. The staff in the first one I came to told me that their computers were down; their directions to another shop down the street proved equally fruitless—it wasn't where they told me it was, or maybe I just didn't understand their Italian. I was now getting off course and a bit anxious. I decided to turn north again in the direction of Monte Sacro to look for a café with Wi-Fi. Ten minutes later I found one and bought an espresso. After logging onto the Internet, I looked up locations for TIM shops on Google Maps and located several within a few kilometers.

I struck out for the nearest TIM shop in the same direction as Monte Sacro, and I found it on the Piazza Euclid in less than twenty minutes of walking. I was relieved that the woman behind the counter spoke excellent English and that her computers were working! Within minutes I was up and running—my SIM card reloaded and my Italian phone number activated. Much relieved, I stepped outside and texted Jane, who by now might be nervous, wondering how I was doing. She texted back almost immediately and then called me.

Chiesa Parrocchiale del Sacro Cuore

My "modern pilgrim's dilemma" solved, I looked at the route on my phone and realized that in all that time I had covered less than five kilometers. Since I was no longer thinking about my phone, I realized that I was hungry and sat down on a bench to eat my sandwich and apple. When I finished eating, I thought I needed a respite from the traffic and noise, so I stepped into the massive Chiesa Parrocchiale del Sacro Cuore, the Parish Church of the Sacred Heart. The quiet, along with the food and the church's peaceful, cavernous interior, provided a welcome break. I was reenergized and ready to resume walking.

THE FINAL 10 kilometers to Monte Sacro took another two hours of walking through the noisy and smelly afternoon rush hour. I soon came to a bike trail, which gave relief from the sidewalks and traffic. I stopped to buy more ice-cold water. The path became quieter as it wound around modern apartment blocks and through thick stands of bamboo that occasionally obscured my surroundings. Joggers and cyclists passed, and the sun sank lower. Coming close to my destination, I chose to leave the path and take a shortcut over a busy bridge, which led me to the street with my hotel. I was relieved to enter the air-conditioned interior and drop my pack.

I was given a small, air-conditioned room by myself, with a single bed and a shower. The woman behind the desk recommended a pizzeria located about a five-minute walk away. After unpacking and showering, I found it just at twilight and got a sidewalk table. The air was pleasantly warm, with a gentle, cooling breeze, and I enjoyed watching the pedestrians passing by. I relished being off my feet and without my pack. An excellent wood-fired pizza and a cold Italian beer topped off my day, and I slept soundly that night.

I was going to need that sleep because the following day I anticipated another day of urban slogging before I entered the open countryside outside of Rome on my way to Monterotondo.

"Angels Unaware" in St. Peter's Square

11

Unexpected Paths

There are no wrong choices, only unexpected paths.

From a sign on the Way of St. Francis

I EXITED the outskirts of Rome the next day, heading north on a sidewalk along a noisy urban highway. It was hot—mid-30s Celsius again—by midmorning, but I had one more errand to complete before I left the city. I needed to stop at an outfitter store—Decathlon—which was in a large shopping area, just a kilometer off my route. Looking at the route, I estimated that I would be there in an hour. The plan appeared to be easy, but I was mistaken.

The detour along a quiet road was easy to find, but what I didn't anticipate was that the shopping mall—just like in the United States—was across an automobile no-man's-land: a highway of fast, four-lane traffic. When I arrived at this junction, I could see the mall, I could see the Decathlon store, just 50 meters away. But this highway was a barrier that was dangerous and tricky to navigate. Ironically, it was even more dangerous than some of the slippery mountain passes I had traversed in Tuscany the previous spring. I wondered what to do: Should I walk another kilometer or two around it? A route on my phone showed me how to do this. Or should I chance crossing it? I was in a hurry, and the hot sun was beating down on me, so I chose to cross where I was, aided by a fortuitously placed construction stoppage that held up traffic just long enough for me to dart across. I entered a parking garage and then the mall. To my relief, it was air-conditioned inside, and I soon found the Decathlon entrance.

The store was packed with locals doing their regular shopping. I suddenly felt self-conscious, dressed in my hiking clothes, with a large pack on my back. Out along the road I had felt like a pilgrim. In here I felt I was a stranger from America doing a strange thing—a pilgrimage. It felt good to be out of the sun and the heat, but I was anxious to get going. I soon found the hiking poles I wanted and also a Swiss Army knife. As I waited in line, I picked up three bottles of ice-cold water to purchase and downed the first two before I was out of the store. Retracing my steps through the mall and the parking garage, I once again crossed the dangerous highway (thank you, road construction!) and eventually regained my route.

The shopping trip, while necessary, had cost me an hour. It was now early afternoon and the day had grown hot. There was no shade on the sidewalk, and I was wishing I had left much earlier in the day. Walking in Italy in September, with its heat, is different from walking in April. In spring, Jane and I had donned light coats at the start of each morning to keep ourselves warm and removed layers as the day wore on and our bodies grew hot from our efforts. I knew in advance that Italy was hot in early September, especially Rome and the hills to its north, and I was concerned about carrying enough water. I had experienced dehydration on hikes and long-distance bike rides and knew the danger. Consequently, as the day wore on, I conserved my water, taking only occasional drinks. But with the hot air, the water in my bottle was getting hotter and less refreshing with each sip

In another half hour, the traffic thinned out and I saw the first waymark on a utility pole for the Way of St. Francis, the *Via di Francesco*. It was pointing north to Assisi! Apparently, going to Assisi from Rome was not so unusual after all. The traffic disappeared entirely as I entered the desolate Marcagliana Nature Reserve on a dirt road. The next two hours I walked under an increasingly hot sun along shadeless, bleak, and dusty roads. The contrast from the first hours could not be greater—no more cars, people, or noise, not even birdsong. I encountered my first pilgrim of this stage, a Dutchman named Jos who was cycling north when he stopped to ask me for directions. I had hoped that at an agriturismo I could replenish my water supply, which by now was getting low, but it was closed when I got there.

I left the preserve and was then into farmland. The harvest here had passed, and the fields were now a lifeless brown, bordered by low, green bush. I stopped under the shade of a tree to eat a sandwich and drink the last of my water. I was thinking that I didn't have too much farther to go when I turned off the dirt road onto asphalt and saw my destination for the day—Monterotondo—atop a hill straight ahead. This was heartening. Looking at my guidebook, I realized that I had only three more kilometers to walk and estimated that I could be there in 40 minutes if I picked up my pace. The road took several turns skirting more brown fields, then turned again to dirt before I came to an impasse: a temporary fence and a flock of sheep. I wondered, *What should I do now?* I found a gate but was worried that the sheep might press through if I opened it. As I wondered about this, a car approached. It was the shepherd. He got out, drove the sheep back, opened the fence, and let me through. I thanked him and then crossed the field to an asphalt road that would take me upward into Monterotondo.

Two kilometers from Monterotondo, visible on top of the hill

I saw that my path led up a very steep and long hill—so steep that I couldn't see the town. The sun was still beating down, and I was hot and dehydrated. After walking for hours I was deflated, but there was nothing to do but climb and try not to think about how much farther I needed to go. Once I got to the top, I reasoned, it would be a short walk into town. Good thing I didn't look at my guidebook, because if I had I would have known that after getting to the top the road descended steeply and swooped up yet again on another very steep hill. When I made this discovery, I stared at this next hill in thirsty disbelief and then dragged myself down and up the final kilometer into town. I stopped in the first shop that I came across and bought two bottles of water that I drank as quickly as I could. I finally found my B&B, where I drank several *more* bottles of cold water and then recovered on the bed—in the air-conditioning!—for a long time before showering and getting enough strength back to venture out for a meal.

MONTEROTONDO IS a delightful bedroom community of about 40,000 people, situated on a hilltop just 25 minutes by train from Rome. Even though I had walked for two days from Saint Peter's and felt like the city was far behind me, I was actually still within its outer suburbs. As the sun went down, the temperatures cooled into the 20s Celsius, and the evening grew pleasant. The streets filled with families pushing strollers and young people out for the *passeggiata*, or evening stroll. I walked the hilly town and its narrow streets for half an hour until I came to the colorful Via Camillo Benso Conte di Cavour, with its long rows of tables under umbrellas filling the street, which was blocked off at that time of evening from vehicles. I checked menus at the various restaurants before I settled on one where I ordered the "specialty," a bowl of *pasta carbonara*, a dish made with bacon and parmesan cheese, perfect after a day of hiking. I also ordered a beer and *acqua frizzante* (sparkling water), since I was still thirsty, and watched the town stroll by. I asked the young woman serving my table if a salad was available, but she said no and suggested instead "broccolini," which sounded a lot like "broccoli," so I ordered it. To my surprise she delivered a large bowl full of something that looked a lot like boiled spinach. I stared at it in despair—this had been my absolutely most disliked dish as a child, and I had not eaten it in over 50 years. I pondered what to do and recalled my Pilgrimage Principle 4: "Accept whatever is offered you, as a gift from God" and Pilgrimage Principle 10: "Appreciate the locals and get to know them. Sample their foods." I actually like *fresh* spinach but have a hard time imagining *boiled* spinach as God's gift.[1] Still, I obeyed and ate. It didn't taste any better than my childhood recollection (boiling having brought out the sharp taste of iron), but I ate it with gratitude, imagining my mother smiling on me from above.

Via Camillo Benso Conte di Cavour

THE NEXT MORNING, I inadvertently picked up a walking companion and my journey took a figuratively unexpected path.

The day had begun with a yogurt, some fruit, and a small espresso on the top deck of my guesthouse, where I was the only guest. Heavy clouds gathered overhead, promising rain. I looked at the weather radar on my phone and saw a heavy band of showers headed my way. I finished eating, gathered up the contents of my pack, and headed into town, looking for a small grocer and a café. At a grocer I wanted to buy sandwiches or fruit; at a café I was hoping for a good Italian pastry and a cappuccino. I didn't find a small grocer, but I did find a café and stopped in just as a downpour started.

I waited 30 minutes while it rained hard. By now it was after 10:00, which was getting pretty late for my planned walk, and I was wishing I could be on my way. I consoled myself that at least I was waiting out the rain in *a town in Italy,* sipping *an Italian cappuccino,* and eating *an Italian pastry.* I thought to myself, *Certainly, worse things could happen.* When the rain lightened, I pulled on my raincoat and headed toward the trail access, which was down the hill. I hadn't gone far before I spied a large supermercato—just what I was looking for. I crossed the road, dodging streams of water coursing along the curb, and went inside in search of a sandwich and fruit. While selecting an apple, I heard a roar on the roof and recognized that the rain had started again, and this time it was a deluge.

I became resigned to wait. I paid for my items, stepped outside the store, and sat down on a bench beneath cover. Water rushed in torrents across the parking lot, and people dashed to their cars under their umbrellas. I looked at the radar app on my phone and could see the band of showers would pass soon—I needed only to be patient and wait.

Out of the corner of my eye, I spied someone with a red backpack. Another pilgrim, wearing shorts and hiking boots! Unmistakable. I had decided in advance that I would stop and greet every pilgrim (Pilgrimage Principle 8: Greet and take interest in other pilgrims; offer them something if they need it), and since I had nowhere to go, I went over to him. He was shorter and slighter than I am, but obviously he was used to hiking. I introduced myself and asked where he was from and where he was going. "Ed," he said, "from Holland." He was going toward Assisi, though he was a bit vague on his route, except that he was destined for Montelibretti, as I was. As I later found out, we even had reservations at the same B&B for that evening.

My doppelgänger, Ed

HE HAD gray hair and a beard and seemed to be around my age—I learned later that he was exactly my age—having just become a "pensioner," off on his first retirement adventure. The beard, the age—he could have been my doppelgänger, except that he had hair on the top of his head.

During the month before departing, I had imagined that this walk would be an opportunity for solitude. However, it was also a pilgrimage, and I needed to "walk in expectation of the unexpected" (Pilgrimage Principle 5). I said I was also going in that direction, and we agreed to walk together once the rain let up. At least for the moment, I was no longer walking solo.

12

The Work of Walking

The difference between the kind of work I do in my early years and the work I do in my later years is obvious. The purpose of retirement is not to free us from working. It is to free us from being chained to it like road gangs to gravel beds. . .. Instead, work is meant to be a fulfillment of our very selves and our purpose for being alive.

Joan Chittister, *The Gift of Years*

I LIKED ED IMMEDIATELY. He had been on adventures around the world, having climbed Mount Kilimanjaro and to the base camp of Mount Everest. Like me, he liked to cycle and had taken long-distance trips via bike as well as on foot. He was a geodetic engineer and very interested in geography and history, two of my interests. I was fortunate that Ed spoke excellent English since I knew no Dutch.

Ed and I turned out to be surprisingly good trekking partners, and what began as just one day's walk together stretched into four, all the way into Rieti. We walked at the same pace and liked the same balance of quiet and conversation. He appreciated stopping to read the historical markers, just as I did. I was writing a book about my journey; he was recording his on a blog. We were different in other ways, though, especially our approaches to food and drink: I marveled at how little water he drank; he marveled at how much I ate. Ed only sipped occasionally out of a flask of ice water during the day, whereas I downed multiple liters and always carried extra. In one of his blog posts he wrote, "Russ thought the breakfast was a bit meager and is eating more. He orders a croissant, two of those very large, triangular sandwiches with hearty toppings, and an espresso at the bar, and it all goes inside too. I don't agree with him. As usual, I don't need much during the day, because apparently I can walk on my body fat and only lettuce at the table in the evening." As a Dutchman, he was characteristically direct, which made him easy to get to know. I appreciated his sense of humor. Sharing a room with me, he discovered that I snored, writing in his blog, "I've found out that Russ can cut pretty good wood at night. But my earplugs hold back most of it, and so I get out of bed at 6:45 a.m. refreshed for a very early breakfast.

WE HEADED out of Monterotondo on a paved bike trail as the rain let up. We crossed paths with the first of several pilgrims that day: a young German woman, dripping wet and shivering, who asked us where town was. We motioned behind us and said it was less than a kilometer. She said she had been unable to find lodging the night before and had spent the night in a barn. We told her that she would be there in 10 minutes before farewelling her with a *"Buon Cammino."*

Before long, the clouds broke, as my radar app had predicted, and the sun came out. Ed put away his umbrella; I peeled off my raincoat. We were soon on quiet paved roads in rolling, green countryside. To the east we could see the higher peaks of the Apennines, while the nearer hills were covered in olive groves and vineyards. This was a rich agricultural region.

We came upon a shady picnic place near a stream and stopped to rest our legs and to eat—for me, a large sandwich, a bun, and fruit; for Ed, some nibbles of chocolate and a few bites of a sausage. A pilgrim from the Czech Republic, on his way to Rome, stopped to greet us. He shared that he had previously walked from home—Pilsen—to Santiago de Compostela, a distance of 3,000 kilometers. He warned us that there was a lot of mud and deep puddles up ahead and looked down dismissively at my Chaco sandals.

He was wearing sturdy ankle-high boots and remarked, "You'll never get through with those. There's a big puddle up ahead." By now I was quite used to people being skeptical about my sandals. Later, after Ed and I found the deep mud and puddles, I noticed that Ed had to spend a lot of time cleaning all the mud off of the soles of his boots, whereas I just swished my feet in the puddles for a few seconds and went on my way, my feet and sandals drying in minutes.

~

ROME TO RIETI crosses through the region of Lazio, a trek of about 110 kilometers. The names of many of the towns in the region contain "Monte" or "Poggio," both of which refer to mountains or hills. It is not surprising then that the route goes up and down constantly, often along rocky paths that double as streambeds in a rainstorm.

Rough paths in Lazio

Occasional heavy rains and their accumulation had washed a lot of soil down from the freshly plowed fields, so we trekked through abundant mud. The lush vistas repeated themselves: more vineyards and olive groves, along with castles and monasteries, and with towns and villages atop each ridge or hilltop. Everywhere was green, green, green. We stopped repeatedly to look at the thick grapevines—the bunches of fruit were huge and ready for harvest, quite a contrast to the sprouts I had seen on the vines in Tuscany five months earlier.

Lazio doesn't have many connections to the life of Francis, but it does have lots of connections to the ancient Romans. Many villages and towns still stand on the foundations of Roman walls. Roman ruins and roads are everywhere in the landscape. The Romans were expert engineers, excelling at building roads that were as straight and flat as possible. They raised their roadbeds on solid stone and finished them with fine gravel. I have walked on the remains of their roads all over Europe. Two thousand years ago these roads radiated outward in all directions from the center of Rome. Initially they were constructed to facilitate conquest but eventually were used for commerce. We crossed a long Roman stone bridge that has stood for 2,200 years, the *Ponte Sambuco* (Elder Bridge). It stands along one of those roads, the *Via Salaria* or Salt Road.[1] Later, we passed a standing Roman milestone, though the carvings on it were long gone.[2] These stones were placed every mile along all Roman roads, engraved with the number of miles to the Forum in ancient Rome.

The restored Church of San Martino in Poggio Moiano

My guidebook said Rome was 40 miles from there along the ancient Via Salaria. It seemed to me that it was much farther, but who was I to argue with the Romans? Ed, amused by my dispute about this distance, wrote in his blog, "We should be much farther from Rome, [Russ] thinks. But yes, he is American and with Americans everything is bigger."

There is mixed memory of the past in these places. One imposing ruin, the so-called Devil's Bridge, stands half overgrown in brush at the top of a ravine, about a kilometer outside Ponticelli. It stands 10 meters high and 40 meters long and is constructed of enormous stone blocks. It isn't clear any longer what it once was—an

Roman milestone Miglio XL

abutment for the Via Salaria? A bridge over an ancient and now vanished stream? The information sign states that the knowledge and memory of the original purpose are lost, but not the fact that this wooded area was notorious for robbery in medieval times, hence the "devil" in the name of the bridge.

The region had a mixed ambience. We saw towns and villages everywhere, so it felt quite inhabited. But our paths took us through quiet countryside, away from traffic, giving a sense of remoteness. The towns we stayed in were small— Montelibretti, Ponticelli, and Poggio San Lorenzo—with few shops or grocers. We feasted on local pastas and vegetables one day and scrounged for a meal the next. The locals were always welcoming and friendly. They were especially generous with wine and beer, as well as grappa, a strong alcoholic drink made from the leftover seeds, stems, and skins of grapes.

Enjoying the local festival in Poggio San Lorenzo with fellow pilgrims Ollie from Switzerland (left) and Renata from Germany (right)

Café in Poggio Moiano

As I walked this stretch of the Way, I reflected on how much this walking had become part of a new and vital vocation for me. In years past, my primary vocation as a book publisher meant that I spent much of my time in front of a computer screen. My energy and creativity were driven into strategy meetings, answering constituents, developing a staff. I traveled a great deal and worked long hours, even as I made every effort to be home for my family. I tried to develop my leadership skills while tending to my own soul, but the demands of my job seemed limitless. I spent 11 years downsizing our publishing agency and that took a toll on me, especially when I had to cut staff, many of whom had become friends. Difficult decisions that have no happy outcomes are taxing. In the end, I downsized myself and "downshifted," meaning that I slowed the pace of my life dramatically.

Taking most of a year off, including walking the 500 miles of the Camino de Santiago, had rejuvenated my soul and my body. I felt gratitude that I still had the stamina to walk 25 kilometers a day and climb these Italian mountains. Years before I would have thought it nuts to arrive in a city, jetlagged, and immediately start walking, but here I was, several days into the adventure. Walking, writing about walking, speaking about walking, encouraging others to try a pilgrimage—that is now what I do, my vocation.

In sacred travel, every experience is uncanny. No encounter is without meaning. There are signs everywhere, if only we learn how to read them.

Phil Cousineau, *The Art of Pilgrimage*

IN MY PREVIOUS WORK, with its busy, over-scheduled life, I would have had a hard time recognizing the "signs" around me, like the one that was there for me as I sat waiting out the rain in front of the COOP in Monterotondo. That "sign" was to greet my fellow pilgrim. I say this because it turned out that I was glad to walk with a companion. While I had walked solo on the Camino de Santiago four years earlier, and appreciated the solitude, with it came loneliness. On that route, loneliness is offset by the large pilgrim community: I often ate meals with the new friends I made, and many of the *albergues*, or pilgrim hostels, served communal meals. The towns and villages are geared toward pilgrims. The Way of St. Francis is different: The pilgrim community is small, and the towns are not specifically stops for pilgrims. As much as I enjoyed the solitude, I realized in the end that I felt fortunate to have found a new friend to walk with.

This is one of the gifts of pilgrimage that comes to us when we are alert and aware of its presence.

Roman inscription preserved in the stonework of Santa
Vittoina

13

Good Morning, Good People

[Francis] opened windows that had long been closed and admitted the air and sun; he banished the sense of gloom that had pervaded Christianity and supplanted it with joy. Up to then the faithful had been taught that their brief span on earth was but an insignificant prelude to eternity and that in this inexorable advance toward this outcome they were but anonymous marchers. Francis did not believe that the prospect of the next world should cloud man's vision of this world; he saw an inherent harmony between the realm of the spirit and the realm of physical reality.

Sarel Eimerl, *The World of Giotto*

RIETI IS the largest city in the valley named after it. In ancient times the valley, 20 kilometers long and 15 kilometers wide, was a bowl, its rivers not having an easy outlet to the Tiber. Ringed on all sides by mountains, in prehistory it had been a lake, its outlets choked off by limestone deposits. Eventually much of the lake was reduced to unhealthy marshland. In 271 B.C.E. the Romans, being good engineers, solved this problem by building a canal and the 165-foot-high Cascata delle Marmore, or Marmore Falls, still the highest manmade waterfall in the world.[1] Once drained, the valley became known for its fertility and as the "Granary of Rome." Today, Lago di Piediluco, or Lake Piediluco, at the northern end of the valley, is the largest of several lakes that are remnants of that ancient lake.

The city of Rieti is situated at the southeast corner of the valley. Francis had come here with a few companions early in his new life as *Il Poverello*. Lacking a positive reception in his hometown, he found a better one in the Rieti Valley and returned there frequently, establishing four sanctuaries in the mountains that encircle the valley. A local path, the *Cammino di Francesco*, links those sanctuaries, part of which is incorporated into the Way of St. Francis. After a dearth of Franciscan-related sights, Ed and I were now surrounded by them.

Ed had planned to take a rest day in Rieti, so we said farewell after dinner, and the following day I headed to Poggio Bustone, the next stage on the way to Assisi. I wasn't sure of my subsequent plans once there, but at the very least I planned to climb to the Grotto of the Revelations, a tiny sanctuary built out from a cave high on the mountainside. I had visited it before, found it deeply moving, and wanted to return there.

THE WALK north to Poggio Bustone was not long—18 kilometers—but it ascended 900 meters as it hugged the eastern edge of the valley. It was on this very section that Jane and I had begun our own pilgrimage to Assisi three years earlier. The memories of that first day came back to me as I exited the city, going at first north, then east along busy main roads, before beginning to ascend on a rural highway. I was only an hour out of Rieti when the road turned onto a wooded trail near the sanctuary of La Foresta. This is one of the few sanctuaries of Francis that is not on top of a mountain. In his time it was the parish church of Saint Fabian, where Francis recovered from an unsuccessful eye surgery in 1224. According to the legend, when the locals heard he was there, they overran the church and ate all of the grapes that the priest had in his vineyard. The priest was disturbed by his loss of grapes, but the story says that Francis miraculously produced an abundance of wine to compensate for it. Today it is a peaceful spot, and the convent is used as a rehabilitation center for people with drug addictions.

Santuario La Foresta

PAST THE SANCTUARY the path heads into thicker woods, and a rocky trail climbs toward Poggio Bustone. I recalled this stretch well from my first time there, and the trail felt like an old friend from there on. I also knew that Francis once walked these very roads. I encountered multiple groups of pilgrims coming the other way: three Italians from near Bari and a group of Europeans and Aussies. Halfway through the day, I stopped to snack in the peaceful garden of San Felice, a small rural church constructed around a miraculous well.[2] Two children were playing soccer in its grassy courtyard. An older Italian couple out on a day's walk presented me with a bunch of grapes.

Another half hour of climbing along asphalt roads brought me to the top of a ridge and an incredible vista, with the Rieti Valley to my left and the high mountain peaks ahead and to my right. I caught a glimpse of Poggio Bustone, seven kilometers ahead, hugging the lower slopes of Monte Rosato, whose dry and rocky crest tops out at over 1,400 meters in elevation. This road undulated past beautiful farms and villas and led to the small town of Cantalice, a vertical town draped at the head of a gorge, one of the most charming spots along the entire Way of St. Francis. Approaching from the south brought me into the upper part of the town. Directly ahead I could see the yellow church of San Felice da Cantalice a Centocelle and the tower of the old castle above it.

When Jane and I went through here in 2019, I was instantly enchanted by this spot. The road brought us right into a narrow *piazza* in front of the church that affords a breathtaking view to the town's center, sixty vertical meters below, which can be reached via a long series of steps. Above the church are the ruins of a castle and the remains of a tower. We had paused and taken photos at this spot, and I had looked longingly at the castle tower at the top of the hill, wishing to go up, but we were too tired. I remembered thinking to myself, *Next time I'm here, I'm climbing to the castle.*

Cantalice with the Torres del Cassero (Tower) on the top

This was the next time. When I saw the sign pointing to the Piazza Castello, I climbed up a steep track that wound around various houses, until I came to the ruins of the castle. I took my time photographing it, especially marveling at the ruins of the tower. I had the sense that I might topple it if I leaned on it too hard. Satisfied that I had seen and photographed all I could, I descended the 350 steps to the central piazza. I went into a café for a drink of cold water and to orient myself to the route out of town, which is a narrow track cut into a steep hillside.

In another hour I was at the base of the mountain below

Poggio Bustone. If Cantalice seems to have settled gently inside the curve of the mountain, Poggio Bustone juts out from the heights, clinging to the mountain above. No matter the angle from which I look at the town—below, above, or inside—I wonder how it hangs on and how they built it. Did they start from above and build downward, or the other way around? Is the bottom holding the top, or the top holding the bottom? Either way, the current town is a maze of homes and shops along steep and narrow alleys that cross the major road, which loops its way repeatedly up the hillside in a series of switchbacks that terminate at San Giacomo, a Franciscan convent founded not long after Francis died, which still serves as a hostel for pilgrims.[3] Standing at the very top of the town, I found myself captivated by the views of the valley that stretch all the way around back to Rieti.

I was tired from the long climb into the town. I had reserved a small guest apartment next to the parish church, and after getting my key I decided to unload my pack, shower, and lie down. My phone was low on power, and as I dug for my charging adapter and cable, my heart sank. I couldn't find it. I took my kit completely apart and still it was nowhere to be found. I sat down and thought about the night before at my B&B in Rieti, and then I could picture where I had left it plugged in: next to the bedside table. I texted the owner and sorted through my options. I still had my battery pack, which would allow me a full charge of the phone and then some, but that would only help me for one more day. I would have to buy another charger in order to continue. In the meantime, I would have to rely on the grace and help of others, made harder by the fact that I was on my own in the apartment. Weighing my options, I decided that I would first go and search for a charger in town, if there was indeed any place where I could find such a thing.

Poggio Bustine

While beautiful, Poggio Bustone is a small town, with one grocer/convenience store. I found nothing to help me there. My original plan had been to hike over the mountain to Piediluco the next day, but I had a problem there too: All the lodging there was full. I also knew that it too was a small town and unlikely to have a shop with what I needed. Right then I heard back from the B&B owner in Rieti—yes, she found my charger. At this point I was tired from the day's trek and the further fruitless search of town. I decided to head back to Rieti the next day and collect the charger and take a day off to collect myself inwardly, which seemed like a good idea. I would spend the next morning in Poggio Bustone, climb to the chapel at the Grotto of the Revelations, and then take a bus back to Rieti.

THE GROTTO, or cave, above Poggio Bustone is famous for two revelations that Francis received there during all-night vigils in prayer. The first was the assurance that the sins of his former life were forgiven. The second is best told by his earliest biographer and contemporary, Thomas of Celano: "He was caught up above himself, and absorbed into a kind of light; the capacity of his mind was enlarged, and he could see clearly into the future. He said to his brothers, 'I saw a great many men who wanted to share our way of life —the roads as it were, filled with Frenchmen, Spaniards, Germans, Englishmen and many others speaking various languages and hurrying toward us.'"[4]

In the morning, I went down the hill to have breakfast in a small café, then climbed back up the hill to San Giacomo, where a trail heads up to the Grotto. The trail is not long— less than one kilometer—but it is very steep, switching back and forth through the forest as it ascends over 300 meters. Carefully positioned along the stone-paved path are seven stone shrines, constructed in the 17th century, large enough that it's easy to mistake one of those for the chapel.

It took me about 20 minutes to climb to the simple stone chapel, which was constructed above the original cave in the first two centuries after Francis. It sits among the treetops on a ledge below a sheer rock face. Of all the special places of

Francis I have visited, I love this one because of its simplicity, its view, its solitude, and because tour busses can't reach it. Since it takes a great deal of effort to get there, few go. The rock face, which rises another 30 or 40 meters above the chapel, is held in check by wire mesh. Pilgrims weave crosses and leave offerings hanging on the wire.

Entrance to the lower chapel

The chapel has two levels; the upper, reached by a short stairway, has a door opening onto a porch. There I laid out seashells from the Chesapeake Bay, and lit two votive candles. I thought the seashells a fitting from my home in Virginia. It was my "offering" and fulfilled Pilgrimage Principle 12: "Leave behind somewhere an appropriate token." Then I went out to the small porch and sat reading and looking over the valley below. I hung more oyster shells on the wire mesh. I breathed in the mountain air, enjoyed the pine scent on the breezes and the amazing view of the treetops and of the valley below. I pictured Francis here 800 years before and recalled those revelations he had supposedly received at this spot. While I don't always believe the legends about Francis, these stories seemed authentic. I saw how the sheer beauty of the place, up above the valley, gave him a virtually "divine" perspective.

After an hour, I slowly made my way back down the steep mountain path. According to the legend, when Francis descended after his revelations, he was so happy that he shouted spontaneously to the locals *"Buongiorno, bene gente!"* or "Good morning, good people!" I wasn't ready to shout, but as I collected my pack and bought my bus ticket to Rieti, I better understood the origin of Francis's exuberant spirit.

Gate to the upper chapel, with its bell tower

14

Poetry in Action

The example of Saint Francis shows how great a place the beauty of the world can have in Christian thought. . . His very choice of places for solitary retreats or for the foundations of his convents was the most beautiful poetry in action. He stripped himself naked in order to have immediate contact with the beauty of the world.

Simone Weil, *Waiting on God*

AFTER RETURNING FROM POGGIO BUSTONE, I took the afternoon in Rieti to ponder what to do next. I had three days before I needed to return to Rome for my flight home. I was clearly not going to Piediluicco, nor all the way to Assisi. I felt that I needed a rest, both physically and inwardly, so I got a room in a hotel for three nights. I thought more about the other two sanctuaries in the Rieti Valley, Greccio and Fonte Colombo. I decided to use my remaining time to explore them, using Rieti as my base.

They were close enough to where I was staying that I could reach them by foot or by train in the mornings (following the local path, the *Cammino di Francesco*) and then use my afternoons to write postcards, record the journey, and let my spirit catch up with my experiences.

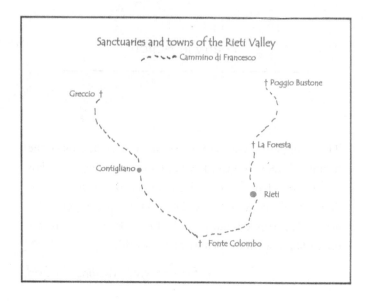

Sanctuaries and towns of the Rieti Valley

Cammino di Francesco

† Poggio Bustone

Greccio †

† La Foresta

Contigliano ●

● Rieti

† Fonte Colombo

GRECCIO STATION, where I began my first day's exploration, is a 10-minute train ride from Rieti and sits among farmland. Leaving the station, I soon found myself on a challenging climb on a quiet, shady asphalt road that rises nearly 300 meters in elevation before it reaches Santuario di Greccio, about four kilometers away. The road was lonely, and I didn't see anyone else until I passed a father and son harvesting grapes in a small vineyard outside their home. I stopped to take a photo of them, and the son, who spoke English, rushed over to hand me a large bunch and said, "These are good to eat and even better for making wine!"

I had seen photos of Santuario di Greccio, but seeing it in person was astounding. Reminiscent of La Verna, the convent rises dramatically out of the rock, as if chiseled out of the mountain itself. A forest frames it on all sides, magnifying its mystique.

Santuario Greccio

Francis had frequented the nearby town of Greccio and loved the people there. In a story reminiscent of La Verna, the original sanctuary was gifted to Francis and the friars from a nobleman. "Lord John of Velita, who held sway over Greccio... gave the mountain, with its series of interconnecting caves, to Francis."[1] I couldn't help thinking again that, while Francis and his friars may not have owned anything, they were given access to some of the most spectacular places for their sanctuaries, which the Franciscan Order came to possess after his death.

The original cave that Francis sought for prayer has since been absorbed inside a Franciscan convent constructed in the 14th century. A self-guided tour took me through the lower portion of the building and past the original, first friars' crude habitations, which were hardly more than caves. The second floor passes a chapel and wooden dormitory also constructed in the 14th century.[2] Throughout are beautiful frescoes, including a simple yet striking one showing Mary holding her breast to the infant Jesus.

Mary nurses the infant Jesus while an anxious Joseph looks on.

The tour exits to a paved porch in front of a 1950s-era church. Greccio remains one of the most popular of the sanctuaries, with a hundred thousand visitors per year, and I talked to a group from Indiana that had recently exited a tour bus and who expressed interest in how to do a pilgrimage on foot.

THE SETTING of the sanctuary is dramatic, but Greccio is more famous because of what happened there in 1223. Wishing to celebrate the poverty of the first Nativity, Francis invited local farmers and shepherds to gather there on Christmas Eve for a live reenactment, complete with manger, Mary and Joseph, and animals. He even deposited a doll in the straw to represent the Christ Child.

The scene realistically combined all of the essential elements of Francis: poverty, peasants, animals, simplicity—while making God and the reality of the incarnation of Jesus authentic. One legend says that he even petitioned the Holy Roman Emperor to declare a moratorium on hunting on Christmas day to spare the animals. I wrote a postcard to my wife saying that the place "exuded peace and serenity, even with a tour bus."

I walked three kilometers along a mountain road to the village of Greccio, where I paused for lunch in a café. I circuited the town, took photos, and then resumed my path along the Cammino di Francesco, descending five kilometers on a rocky path to the valley floor to the town of Contigliano, where I caught a local train back to Rieti.

Spending most of his life out of doors, in all seasons, his vision of man's place in nature and the universe was as intense and apocalyptic as William Blake's or Walt Whitman's.

Adrian House, *Francis of Assisi: A Revolutionary Life*

THE NEXT DAY I headed out on foot toward the last of the sanctuaries of the Rieti Valley, Fonte Colombo, 11 kilometers round-trip. The route leaves the city on a pleasant pedestrian/bike route alongside the Velino River before briefly following a shoulderless and very busy highway. After that risky stretch,[3] the route turned onto a quiet dirt road. Once in the woods, the walk led upward along a short, steep, and very stony path.

Fonte Colombo means "fountain of the birds" and is so

named because Francis (who loved birds in particular) saw doves drinking out of a spring there. I found the original spring—still spouting water—after about 15 minutes of hiking through a dense and damp green forest. I continued upward for a few minutes more, then reached the stone-paved entrance of the sanctuary.

My guidebook about the sanctuaries of the Rieti Valley described it this way: "Fonte Colombo [is] a special place. Clinging to the escarpment of the small mountain over-looking the Rieti Valley, one can sense there a special presence. Francis loved this place. As a guest of the Farfa [monks], he found a little chapel dedicated to Saint Mary called Magdalene... it's one of those little churches where Francis loved to lose himself."[4]

It was quiet when I arrived—the only other person I saw was a man with his dog. The complex was simple: a church with a small convent and cloister, and two smaller chapels: Mary the Magdalene and Saint Michael the Archangel. The church was decorated modestly, with a single nave of white plaster, first constructed in the 13th century and expanded over the next two centuries. I encountered a beautiful portrait of the Madonna and Child from the 14th century, but what appealed to me most were the more recent and more mystical stained-glass windows, with scenes from the life of Francis. On the wall was a copy of Francis's Rule of 1223,[5] which he wrote here toward the end of his life, and which created the organizing principle of the movement that would succeed him after his death. Next to the church was the original friary, built for the early Franciscans.

Fonte Colombo was also the place where Francis underwent a medical procedure in 1225, the last year of his life. Never healthy, he had picked up an eye disease when he had traveled in 1218 to preach to the Sultan during the Crusades. Modern scholars think it was possibly trachoma, which caused excessive tearing and blurred vision. An experimental treatment at the time was to cauterize the veins along the side of the eyes with a searing poker, intended to stop the flow of tears and pus into the eyes. The treatment sounds awful, and it must have been so in reality, though the legends about Francis say that he suffered no pain. Either way, the treatment failed, tragically, and he was likely blind when he died.

Down two flights of steps from the church, alongside a deep crevice in the rock, was another of Francis's caves—called *Sacro Speco*. This spot is high on a cliff face (where else?) and it was said Francis maintained a fast here during Lent in 1223 when he composed his final Rule.

St. Michael's, constructed over the crevice, features a thick glass window in the floor looking down into it. A set of metal stairs wound down around the cliff, outside and below the chapel. I came to the crevice—maybe 4 meters long—and walked through.

In the middle I looked upward through the glass and

into the chapel and noticed the stairs carved into the rock; obviously at one point the chapel and the crevice were connected directly.

A fissure in the rock. A cave. A perilous cliff. Why was Francis drawn to these places? In the silence that was partly inside the earth, open to the elements outside, it was safe, quiet, peaceful. I wondered if the energy of the earth, the energy of the rocks, moved him.

I emerged at the other end and stood outside on a walkway. Looking north, I could see the city of Rieti, about five kilometers away. Francis would have seen this, albeit a smaller city in the 13th century. Above me was a sheer rock face that merged into the exterior walls of the chapel, which was a random mixture of stone and clay brick. For a moment I was puzzled: What was built by human hands, and what was here originally? I thought to myself, *Stones are old, but they were themselves created by geologic action over millions of years. They are created perhaps by sedimentation or volcanic action, the pressure and heat of the earth, the living power of its core. They were once alive.* I mused how humans took that creation, the rocks that at first seemed lifeless, and hewed them into shapes, then stacked and combined them into something else entirely, creating a wall or a building. I looked closely at the cliff and noticed lichens and green ferns. In the small cracks and crevices soil accumulated and new life sprouted—stone on stone—humans and nature forming, shaping, evolving, all part of a seamless whole.

The simple chapel of Mary Magdalene

I ended my contemplation of the rocks and slowly took the steps back up to the chapel of Mary Magdalene. This chapel already existed at the time of Francis—a rarity among his sanctuaries—and it has remained unchanged since then. I stepped inside and sat alone and uninterrupted for a long time. The walls contained the remains of frescoes from various periods, including some dating to the 12th century, so I imagined Francis gazing at them. Several small windows were set into the thick walls, and alongside one of those deep insets was a red tau cross purported to have been drawn by Francis himself.

Interior of chapel of Mary Magdalene.

I looked at the red stone floor, interrupted partway by rough white limestone, and imagined that it was the same floor he had stood on. I stepped out of my sandals and stood on the cool floor in my bare feet. I wanted contact with the stone, the same stone that may have touched Francis's feet. I wasn't expecting anything magical or miraculous to happen; rather, I just wanted to sense what he sensed: the cool, smooth floor. The paths, the dirt, the stone—I understood that these were the elements of Francis's Italy, and I wanted to experience them with all my senses. Taking off my sandals was also a way to "strip myself bare" in a Franciscan sort of way, in the place he might have stood.

I SPENT MORE time walking the grounds as the morning wore on and then returned to Rieti on foot, with a deeper understanding of Francis and his places of solitude. La Foresta, Poggio Bustone, Greccio, and Fonte Colombo, even La Verna—I had now experienced them all. While some of his sanctuaries are famed for a miraculous event in his life, I came away thinking more about their original purpose: places of solitude and spiritual refreshment. A more recent biographer, Adrian House, wrote of Francis's ability to connect with people: "[H]e certainly exhibited an exceptional ability to engage people's spirits with God and each other, so that their capacity for love and their will to help others was constantly strengthened... [H]is inspiration appealed to the deeper dimension of their souls...[H]e and his friars exerted their moral influence through an unassuming metaphysical light rather than the ostentatious fire of the zealous."[6]

A 20th-century monk and hermit, Thomas Merton, gave me an even deeper appreciation for the value of these places of solitude for Francis and his brothers: "One of the best things for me when I went to the hermitage was being attentive to the times of the day: when the birds began to sing, and the deer came out of the morning fog, and the sun came up – while in the monastery, summer or winter, Lauds is at the same hour. The reason why we don't take time is a feeling that we have to keep moving. This is a real sickness. Today time is commodity, and for each one of us time is mortgaged. We experience time as unlimited indebtedness. We are sharecroppers of time. We are threatened by a chain reaction: overwork– overstimulation– overcompensation– overkill... We must approach the whole idea of time in a new way. We are free to love. And you must get free from all imaginary claims. We live in the fullness of time. Every moment is God's own good time, his *kairos*. The whole thing boils down to giving ourselves in prayer a chance to realize that we have what we seek. We don't have to rush after it. It is there all the time, and if we give it time it will make itself known to us."[7]

PART III

Rieti to Assisi, September 2019

140 kilometers
3000 meters elevation

15

The Green Heart of Italy

I am proposing a way of looking not only *at* but *through* the road, through our moments of travel to their past and future dimensions, to consider each encounter as a chapter in a long novel, each person along the way as one of the characters in our soul journey through life.

Phil Cousineau, *The Art of Pilgrimage*

I WAS PRETTY sure we were lost. It was early afternoon and an hour since I'd seen a sign for the trail. Jane and I had been walking for four hours, and what seemed like a straightforward hike over a mountain pass had become anything but.

This was our first go at the Way of St. Francis in September 2019, before the pandemic. Jane and I were heading northward on day four of this "test" of sorts, from Rieti to Assisi, a distance of 140 kilometers. We planned seven days of walking, with a rest day in the middle. I created this itinerary believing it involved less climbing, was less remote, and had more towns to stop in than the southward route out of Florence. If we liked it, we would return in a few months and walk the rest of the route. We had booked all our lodging in advance, and if everything went smoothly, we would arrive in Assisi on September 30. The plan seemed perfect.

But there were problems from the start. Our first day, from Rieti to Poggio Bustone, was harder than I had imagined, with much more elevation than we expected. Plus, since we were walking in the opposite direction from what was suggested by the guidebook, we were going to have to rely on GPX navigation.[1] Descriptions of roads and turns made no sense when traveling in the opposite direction. I also discovered that signage was neither always reliable nor, in some cases, even readable.

My phone had the GPX maps and routes on it, but on this leg of the journey it had a problem pinpointing where I was. The blue dot that always, in theory, knows where on Earth you are, seemed to lag, by hours, from my position. Or it might jump and put me on top of a mountain kilometers to the west. Or east. So, phone navigation was no help.

Consequently, we took longer to get to our destination the first day and arrived pretty tired. We decided to take a bus on day two. From our next stop—Piediluco—the route was flat and easy along the Nera River. We arrived after day three in Macenano and had a good night's sleep. Ahead was a climb over a mountain pass followed by an easy descent into Spoleto, where we would enjoy the beautiful city and take an extra day to rest and explore. The distance was 20 kilometers, the elevation 700 meters. I'd done something similar a year earlier when I crossed the Pyrenees from

France to Spain on the Camino de Santiago and felt confi-
dent that we could tackle it.

Entering Macenano

OUR START that day was promising. We ate a large
breakfast, then loaded up with extra food from the hotel
before we left in the cool of the morning. We crossed the
Nera River after an hour and a half of level walking and
went through the small village of Ceselli, where we met a
man who spoke English and told us that our route was
straight ahead up a shady asphalt road. Above us we could
see the green and craggy mountains through which we were
headed. The start of the ascent was relatively easy, as we
climbed past isolated homes and watched the mountain
grow nearer. All seemed well.

Then, around noon, we entered a small settlement that
was not on my guidebook map. Had we made a wrong turn?

I looked the map on my phone, but it was still no help—the blue dot was back at the Nera River. Jane took a break in the shade, and I went back down the road, looking for the missed turnoff. I stopped at a farmhouse and knocked on the door, but no one answered. I knocked on another, and a young man answered, but he spoke no English. I pointed back up the road and asked, "Via di Francesco? Spoleto?" He said something in Italian that I didn't understand and was of no further help. I decided that it would be pointless to ask again, so I said *"Grazie"* and went back up the road to where Jane was sitting.

This muddle had cost us an hour, the sun was getting high, and the air was getting uncomfortably warm.

"I don't know," I said, "but I don't think we've missed a turn. Let's keep on." We went up the road about 30 meters, and there the road started to switchback up the mountain.

After a few minutes I saw another small settlement ahead, which also didn't seem to be on the map. I again looked at my phone for help, but it was still no use. The shade that we had walked in earlier was now gone, and the sun was beating down hard on us.

At this point I was feeling like maybe we were lost. I uttered a short prayer for help.

I looked at the map in my guidebook again. Turning back didn't seem to make sense, *and* I didn't want to head back *down* the switchback. We'd already lost enough time, were running low on water, and needed energy for the climb that I knew was still ahead. I figured that if there were houses ahead, we could ask for help.

We continued heading upward for another five minutes, around yet another sharp turn in the road, when I spied a signpost for the Way of St Francis! It marked the turnoff to a dirt trail heading off the asphalt. In spite of our disorientation, we had found the route. I quietly said a prayer of thanks.

Now that we were certain we were on the right track, I became aware of a second problem: dehydration. We still had several hours of walking over the mountain pass and only a liter of water left between us. I wondered if I should head back to that last farmhouse and ask for more water, but the trip down and back would take at least 45 minutes. We decided to keep going and headed up the narrow, steep, and rocky trail.

Right then, a couple of Cammino Angels appeared, the only hikers we had seen so far that day: a mother and her adult daughter. Surprisingly, they were Americans from California who had come down the trail from Spoleto, which meant they must have left early. *Very early.* More amazing, they asked us if we needed water—each had a heavy CamelBak, and they wanted to unload what they didn't need. How did they guess? Jane and I each filled our extra bottles with two liters of water, enough to get us over the pass and down the mountain. We thanked the women, wished them *"Buon*

Cammino," and walked on, still absorbing what had just happened. And we uttered yet another prayer of thanks.

THE GIFT of water was more than just hydration: As we climbed higher, no longer worrying, we could pause to enjoy the breathtaking views back to the Nera Valley, vistas that many say are the most beautiful and dramatic along the entire Way of St. Francis.

AFTER WE REACHED the mountain pass, we stopped to eat our lunch, quite relieved. It was downhill from there.

After two more hours we descended—quite fatigued—to Monteluco, a Franciscan convent established by Francis in 1218—once again above a cave. By then, it was late afternoon, and I could see that the sun was going to set in an hour, and we were going to need more than an hour to get to the city. I was concerned about walking in the dusk with our poor navigation and fatigue. The area around the convent was parklike, and a few people were walking dogs. I wanted to explore the place but was more concerned about getting to Spoleto. I checked a sign at the bus stop and learned that a bus had just left and there would not be another one until after dark. I approached a few people, asking *"Parli inglese?"* But they all shook their heads. No English.

Just then, another Cammino Angel, Fabrizio, came to our rescue. He had driven up from Rome with his wife and son and had noticed us. Walking across the parking lot, he asked us in English if we needed help. I was surprised—and relieved—to find someone who I could communicate with. I told him that we had just crossed the mountain and were still trying to get to Spoleto that night and were worried about walking the path in the dark. He nodded his head in understanding and said he might be able to help. On our behalf he approached several people nearby and asked them (in Italian) if any of them were going to Spoleto. A woman walking her dogs said she was and offered us a ride. I was amazed again, both at our luck and at the timing, as well as the generosity and helpfulness that came our way. I thanked Fabrizio profusely, climbed in the woman's car, and in minutes (instead of hours) we were in the center of the city, near our lodgings, just before the sun set.

It had been a long and challenging day, but our gratitude for how we had been helped by strangers reminded me —as if I needed reminding—that we were on not just a hike but a pilgrimage and that making ourselves vulnerable to the help of others was the essence of what it means to be a pilgrim.

The stories about such a saint and his companions breathe the subtle perfume of wildflowers. They conjure up memories of the Umbrian valley with its rocky hermitages, its twisting streets on the hilltops, its poplar trees, its sunbathed vineyards and La Verna rising up out of the morning mist. A procession of his followers moves before our eyes sheltering in some shed or poor little abandoned church, men who seemed to have absorbed from Francis some special Franciscan gift of soul.

Hugh McKay, *The Little Flowers of St. Francis*

TWO DAYS after that perilous climb over the mountain into Spoleto, Jane and I were on a path to Trevi, walking through the vast region of olive groves in the central Umbrian Valley. In another two days we would be arriving in Assisi. The air was delightful; gentle breezes welcomed and cooled us as we enjoyed easy dirt roads, with plenty of places to stop and refresh ourselves. At this stage of the route, the hills to climb were few and gentle.

It was midafternoon as I sat on a rock to rest my feet when the familiar scent of oregano wafted up to me. In Italy, the aromatic herbs are everywhere, the roadsides bordered with rosemary, lavender, and dill, as well as oregano. Even the mountain passes are littered with wild thyme. Breathe deeply when you are there: The air of the countryside, not just the food, is seasoned.

Trevi on its hilltop

Umbria is known as *Il cuore verde d'Italia*, or the "Green Heart of Italy,"[2] and its beauty is enchanting. Spoleto—which we had just left—is at the southern end of the Valley of Umbria, which stretches 50 kilometers north to Perugia and Assisi. From Spoleto, the Way of St. Francis skirts the eastern edge of this valley, an easier route that never climbs back up into the steep mountains again.[3] This meant that our last days into Assisi were spent walking through towns and villages along the valley floor or through olive groves on peaceful hillsides. We spent our evenings in two beautiful hilltop towns, Trevi and Spello, with their winding, twisting streets.

The daytime temperatures were not too hot and water stops were frequent, making for more comfortable walking. The evenings were cool, with refreshing breezes blowing through the outdoor restaurants where we ate our late Italian suppers.

The outline of Mount Subasio

Walking northward along the edge of the valley, we also no longer had a problem with navigation, because we could actually see where we were going. Mount Subasio, the home of Assisi, grew larger in our view the whole way, and by the time we arrived at Trevi, the setting sun made Assisi—25 kilometers ahead—sparkle like a white jewel. Looking back from where we had come, Spoleto also gleamed. I had a momentary sense of what Francis might have seen 800 years ago as he trod these very hills, these same cities in front of or behind him.

. . .

THE LAST TWO days along the edge of the valley were wonderful days to walk, with temperatures just warm enough that we never needed jackets. The thing that struck us as we approached Assisi from the south was the sheer accumulation of beauty—beauty of the countryside and the way the setting sun lights up the mountain towns with their ochre and white limestone.

Olives ready for harvest.

The closer we came to Assisi, the more I comprehended that the essence of Francis is in the countryside. We love him for how he loved this world: the people, the land, the flowers, the stones, the birds, the domestic and wild animals. He loved to be outdoors. He loved the touch of the earth, the feel of the wind against his face, the view out over a valley from a height. Now that we were in his home country, we felt it. The wide Umbrian Valley—wilder, less inhabited in Francis's time—this was the vista of his home, the territory he traversed continually. Like him, this undulating path lifted us out of ourselves to something greater.

> We speak of God and geniuses and heroes and sacred sites, but these are only names for the ineffable mystery of the force behind something our souls long to be in touch with.
>
> Phil Cousineau, *The Art of Pilgrimage*

As we entered the final approach to Assisi, it occurred to me that, although I was looking forward to arriving, it was not about the destination, it was not about the bones of a

saint. To be on movement through a sacred landscape—that
is a gift of pilgrimage.

*A defeated Francis returns from his imprisonment in Perugia. This bronze
sculpture is in Spello, but an identical one is on the lawn in front the the
Basilica of Saint Francis in Assisi.*

16

Mystical Assisi

There are some places in the world where one is mysteriously magnified on arrival by the emotions of all those who have arrived and departed before.

Cees Nooteboom, *Roads to Santiago*

When the last tourist bus has rumbled out of the car park and dusk descends over Assisi, an atmosphere of serene mysticism and deep inner peace once more prevails, and regardless of one's faith, this is the perfect place to end a pilgrimage.

Derry Brabbs, *Pilgrimage: The Great Pilgrimage Routes of Britain and Europe*

TIME STANDS STILL IN ASSISI. With its medieval history preserved in stone, it has held onto its charm. Two kilometers long from end to end, the city juts out along a spur of Mount Subasio, itself a massive bulge breaking out of the Apennine chain. Its silhouette is visible at a distance of up to

50 kilometers from both Gubbio in the north and Spoleto in the south. The city's narrow, stone streets twist upward and downward but rarely on the level. The remains of its two castles, the Rocca Maggiore and Rocca Minore, keep watch from above like sentinels, remnants of the town's violent past. The region of Umbria, including Assisi, sits on a seismic fault line, but 800 years ago it also sat at the fault line of a power struggle between the Pope and the Holy Roman Emperor, who at the time was German. This is an important context in which to understand Francis.

The central piazza, virtually unchanged since Francis' time. The Torre del Commune, left, towers over the Roman Temple of Minerva.

ASSISIUM WAS FIRST SETTLED by the Romans over 1,200 years ago, but its history goes back to the Etruscans and their tribal predecessors, the Umbrians. Its central piazza was once the Roman forum, and dominating it is the Torre del Commune, the tall tower constructed in the 13th and 14th centuries. Immediately next to it is the ancient pagan Temple of Minerva (later converted into a church), whose fluted Corinthian columns stand as a reminder of its Roman past. Bracketing the town at each end are its two most beautiful churches, dedicated to its most famous children: the Basilicas of Saint Francis and Saint Clare, each lustrous with a mixture of pink and white limestone cut from Mount Subasio. Assisi is a UNESCO World Heritage Site with three million visitors a year and is, after Rome, the most-visited spiritual destination for pilgrims and tourists in Italy.

Like its streets, its history twists in paradoxes, contradictions, and intrigues. Before 1200, when Francis was still a young man, the city declared itself a *commune* or independent city-state. It tore down the emperor's castle (the *Rocca*) and expanded its defensive walls to protect the small city. Francis himself may have helped construct those walls, learning a skill that would later come in handy. It was out of this foment of independence that Assisi—after casting out and expropriating the property of the ruling nobles—came into conflict with neighboring Perugia (its perennial rival), which had offered refuge to those same wealthy and powerful aristocrats. In that conflict, a young and brash Francis rode out of the city, dressed confidently in a suit of armor, only to be taken prisoner in a brief and disastrous battle after which he spent nearly two years imprisoned. He was to return to Assisi a different young man.

THE CITY also contains further paradoxes: Jesus is quoted in the Gospels as having said (regarding himself) that "A prophet is not without honor, except in his hometown." Francis and Clare may provide an exception to that—they are now honored all over town. Those two, who once scandalized and then were rejected by their home city, are now its chief attractions. As Franciscan writer and teacher Richard Rohr writes, "A supreme irony I want to mention… is that Francis and Clare, two dropouts who totally spurned the entire success, war, and economic agendas of thirteenth-century Assisi, have now been fully sustaining its economy for eight hundred years through the pilgrims and tourists who pour into this lovely medieval town."[1]

The economics of sainthood are an open secret of religious pilgrimage: Pilgrims bring in a lot of money. In the Middle Ages, constructing a shrine or cathedral to house the remains or relics of a saint brought an economic boon. A related irony is that Francis, knowing the end of his life was near, expressed a wish to die in his beloved "motherhouse," the Porziuncola, a small church just outside of Assisi. The man who embraced nonviolence was transported home via a circuitous route, protected by armed but well-meaning knights, to prevent neighboring Perugia (of all places) from snatching him and, after he died, raising a basilica *there* in his honor while boosting their own coffers for decades to come.

ASSISI IS WORTH LINGERING IN. We spent several leisurely days there, walking the coursing streets, taking in its heights and boundaries, sticking our nose into art galleries, cafés, and *panetteria* (bakeries) as well as tourist shops. Of course we took in the famous basilicas of Francis and Clare, as well as other lesser-known places that made Francis and his city famous and endearing. With 28 churches, the town resounds with the frequent chiming of bells.

The Basilica of Saint Francis

On the day they arrive, most pilgrims head to the resplendent Basilica of Saint Francis, located at the northern edge of the city. For anyone accustomed to the pilgrimage to Santiago de Compostela, the process of arrival in Assisi and obtaining a certificate of pilgrimage—a *testimonium*—is anticlimactic. There are no crowds of cheering pilgrims falling on their knees in celebration of arrival. The arrival at the northern and southern gates—Porta Nuova and Porta San Giacomo—were rewarding for us, but no one congratulated us on our achievement. Walking through town with backpacks, we were unusual. Assisi is crowded with tourists and pilgrims who may have arrived via bus or car or train, but it is not crowded, like Santiago, with streams of pilgrims carrying backpacks.[2]

An office below the Basilica of Saint Francis provides the testimonium, and those who have arrived on foot can attend a special evening mass for pilgrims. We attended, though since it was in Italian, I was only barely able to follow. Jane, who grew up Catholic, followed it much better, since she knew the liturgy and could easily figure out what was being said. I just drank in the atmosphere and relaxed in the accomplishment of walking there.

When the site for the basilica was chosen, it sat well below the ancient city walls of Assisi, on the brow of *Colle del Paradiso* (translates as "Hill of Heaven," but it is known as "Hill of Hell"[3]) before it descends into the plains below. The long road to it from the central piazza, nearly a mile long, is lined with shops selling religious souvenirs (especially the olive-wood tau crosses). Maybe it was the setting, but I found these more tasteful than the numerous trinket booths of Rome.

The basilica is simultaneously restrained and gorgeous, both medieval and timeless. It is actually two churches: one built over the other. Constructed in record time—mimicking the record time of Francis's beatification, or first steps toward sainthood—the lower church enshrines his mortal remains below the altar, and both it and the upper church contain some of the most priceless pre-Renaissance frescoes in Italy. *Il Poverello* wanted a simple grave at his beloved Porziuncola, but Pope Gregory IX had other plans.

Standing inside the basilica, I couldn't dismiss its beauty; I tried to see it as the affection showered upon Francis, even after his death, by the town that ultimately embraced him and his movement. They could not forget him—nor he, them. In that sense, I could appreciate it. On the other hand, I recognized that it directly contradicts everything Francis lived for. It remains for me one of Assisi's paradoxes and mysteries: the simple expression of love, from a town that originally rejected him because he turned his back on wealth and property. Strolling through the basilica, I decided that its beauty is what I would remember, and I chose to leave behind my judgments about it.

The same thing can be said about Clare's church, which mirrors Francis's basilica in outward beauty and style, its exterior faced with alternating and distinctive stripes of white and pink limestone. It holds Clare's remains, placed under the high altar nearly 30 years after Francis was interred. Hanging in the side chapel is the original cross of San Damiano before which Francis prayed in the beginning of his ministry. As the story goes, it was the Christ upon this crucifix who spoke to Francis and told him to rebuild the ruined church of San Damiano. The expression on the face of Christ is mysterious: a paradoxical mixture of sadness and resignation or, perhaps, determination.

He had rejected the economic system of calculated wealth: without the anger of a protester, and without condemning a single soul. If he had only this one aspect of his character, it might well mark him for heroic sanctity... Unlike so many devout people, he knew not how to condemn. Neither aggressive nor intolerant, he was a peacemaker and reconciler who open-mindedly admitted almost everyone who came to join the Lesser Brothers.[4]

Donald Spoto, *Reluctant Saint: The Life of Francis of Assisi*

LESS THAN A HUNDRED meters below the central piazza is an important sight that is easily overlooked unless the pilgrim knows the full story of Saint Francis: the Palazzo Vescovile (the bishop's palace), next to a church, the Chiesa di Santa Maria Maggiore. It was here, in the courtyard of the palace in the winter of 1205, that Francis made his decisive break with his family, with their wealth and security, and initially with the town of Assisi itself. As a pilgrim, for me this place—not the basilica, not Francis's tomb—became my ultimate destination within the city walls of Assisi.

The courtyard of the Bishop's Palace

Francis had gone off to the war with Perugia at age 20, dreaming of the glories of battle, but instead he spent up to two years languishing in captivity. That time marked the start of his conversion. Returning home, he was less interested in carousing with his companions, and he lost interest in his father's lucrative business. A further attempt at being a knight and achieving greatness in warfare was suddenly abandoned. He became aimless.

The most popular stories of Francis's conversion culminate with him dismounting from his horse and kissing a leper, the most despised class of society. He subsequently made a pilgrimage to Rome where he exchanged his luxurious clothes for those of a beggar. He fell strangely in love with the idea of material poverty, a poverty rooted in a love of God, a love modeled by Jesus himself. Wealth and riches suddenly became obstacles to attaining this love. Joining his father's business became an impossibility.

Once again home, Francis began to secretly sell his father's wealth—jewels and cloth—giving the proceeds to lepers. This landed him in trouble with his father, Pietro. Francis stole away into the countryside for safety and solitude and hid out in the broken-down church of San Damiano where his most consequential and mystical experience occurred. Looking up at the painted crucifix

Statue of Francis's parents outside his home. A broken chain represents his break with his family.

hanging above the altar, he saw Jesus' lips move and heard the crucified image say to him "Rebuild my church." He took the vision literally.

Secretly returning home, he took more goods from his father, selling them to obtain stones to rebuild the church and paying the priest in charge at San Damiano to keep an oil lamp lit. That was the limit for his father. He imprisoned Francis in his own home and locked him in a cellar, but his mother, Pica, took pity and released her son.[5]

Here the drama reached its peak. Pietro, embarrassed and humiliated by Francis's behavior, decided he had but one choice left: to publicly disown his son. He dragged Francis to the bishop's palace and demanded justice. He wanted back the money that Francis had given the priest, which the bishop now had. Failing to receive it, he sought to publicly and officially disown Francis. Before his father could complete his case, Francis disappeared into the bishop's home and disrobed. Clutching his clothes in his arms, with the bag of coins on top, he returned naked to the bishop's courtyard, and in front of all those assembled he handed the clothes and money to his father, saying "I give these back to you. From now on I have one father, the Father in Heaven."

Francis's father was speechless, his mother was in tears. Still angry, Pietro received the clothes and money, and then he and grief-stricken Pica disappeared from the historical record.

Not so Francis.

Bishop Guido, either in a gesture of modesty or in a symbol of protection, removed his own robe and placed it over Francis. Today the place is marked by a statue that stands in the middle of this courtyard, next to the *Santuario della Spogliazione,* or "Room of the Stripping."

REJECTED by Assisi and wearing a simple peasant's tunic, Francis wandered north to Gubbio before returning and taking up his commission to "rebuild" the broken-down church of San Damiano. He begged for stones and worked at first alone, but he was eventually joined by some of his former friends. Thus began a further scandal, as one after another of these young men—the cream of Assisi's society —turned their back on privilege and joined Francis. A movement was born.

The next years and decades found Francis reluctantly leading a religious order. This was not his plan, but the times were rife with religious dissenters and nonconformists, most of whom, unfortunately, ended their lives burned at a stake for heresy. Maybe the greatest miracle of Francis—and here I do see it as a miracle—was that this was not his fate. He instead received the blessing of Pope Innocent III. He pledged his followers to personal poverty—the renunciation of property, power, and money—as well as to chastity and service to the poor. This was all in imitation of and according to the teachings of Jesus—which, ironically, the Church no longer universally embraced. Francis traveled throughout Italy, preaching in the towns and villages to the common people. His heartfelt care for everyone, his dedication to peace, sprang from a deep connection between his spirit and God. The flame of his spirit was like a match that lit a fire across Europe. Within a decade, thousands joined him, at first men, but later women, through Clare. Later Francis founded a third order of married men and women, and those three orders have remained steadfast through history.

When you agree to live simply, you have *time* for spiritual and corporal works of mercy because you have renegotiated in your mind and heart your very understanding of time and its purposes. Time is *not* money anymore, despite the common aphorism. Time is life itself.[6]

Richard Rohr, *Eager to Love*

IN REJECTING both money and power. Francis abandoned the recognized economic system, and it ceased to exert power over him. Possessing nothing, Francis paradoxically lived a life of abundance.[7] He and his friars begged, but unlike panhandlers they often worked alongside the local peasants, accepting only food for payment, and even that without demanding it. His nonviolence was rooted in his poverty, as he famously said: "If my friars had possessions, it would require them to have weapons to defend them."

His embrace of "Lady Poverty," as he called it, came at a critical junction in history. As Donald Spoto recognized:

> Precisely at this time, money was becoming more than simply a social convention[,] a medium of economic exchange. People were beginning to pursue money as a primary goal; and the amount of money one acquired determined one's status in the community. Society in the 21st century in fact operates on the same tacit assumption that began in the 13th—namely that money can indeed buy happiness or at least rent it. . . . Francis's era was the first time in history, since the Roman Empire, that costly items were purchased for no other purpose than to publicize the surplus wealth of the owner—and these items were, for the most part, clothing. Expensive garments were identified with status, and status with social importance. People began to know the price of a great deal, but the real value of very little. Thus began what Thorstein Veblen, 700 years later, famously termed "conspicuous consumption."[8]

17

Farewell to Francis

Who asks not life but only place to die.

Gerard Manley Hopkins, "A Fragment of
Anything You Like"

ASSISI IS HARD TO LEAVE. The mountain air, the twisting streets with their medieval mystique, are hard to let go of. Both times we arrived we were also completing a pilgrimage, and completing a pilgrimage means going home. Leaving a pilgrimage is itself also hard.

Arriving twice on foot, we departed twice on foot for the train station, a four-kilometer walk down to the valley floor. The station is in the sizable town of Santa Maria degli Angeli, or Saint Mary's of the Angels. It stands out prominently as you look over the valley from Assisi because of the massive basilica there by the same name. We stopped there before we left town.

But first, downhill just a kilometer from Assisi is the

equally famous San Damiano. The walk down to the station can be taken past San Damiano. It can be visited separately or as a stop on the way out of town.

In Francis's time, San Damiano was a ruin—a disused chapel. It is where he had a vision of Christ speaking to him from the cross, saying "Rebuild my church." I imagined him finding solace among its piles of stones, a sharp contrast to the massive fortress above the city and the tall towers of the wealthy merchants like his father.

The peaceful cloister of San Damiano

The people of the city considered him a fool when he began the chapel's reconstruction. However, he attracted the curious—including some former friends—and it was here that the first friars joined him, including some of those friends. The completed church became a place he returned to repeatedly, and when Clare joined him and started her associated order of Poor Clares, he secured them this place. Clare would have preferred an itinerant life like Francis's, but the Roman Catholic Church would only sanction women living in enclosed convents, and this is what Clare and her sisters did. They remained there until seven years after her death in 1253. For the next several centuries the place changed hands—from Franciscan to private owner-ship—until about 40 years ago, when it was donated back to the church and once again became a small Franciscan convent. We found it to be our second-favorite place in Assisi, after the courtyard of the bishop's palace.

The walk to San Damiano is through groves of old olive trees, weathered and twisted into marvelous shapes, and it is easy to imagine it this way 800 years ago. The building is simple, with a cloister and the original church.

We stopped there on the feast day of Saint Francis, October 4, but surprisingly it was not crowded with tourists. Before entering we gazed back up at the city, where people were busy celebrating Francis, and imagined him standing where we were, gazing up at Assisi as he began his solitary work of reconstruction. From down here, Assisi felt like a different world. The cloister—traditionally the place for contemplation—was full of red geraniums; it was unassum-ingly beautiful. The interior of the church was modest, and upon entering I looked long at the stones, thinking of the fact that Francis had placed them there. The brilliant deco-rations of the basilica above were missing here—the atmosphere was subdued and calm, with a more "Franciscan" feel. I liked what my local guidebook said: "Poverty, simplicity, peace, reign sovereign. Many of the pages of Franciscan life, as described in the early biographies of the saint, still seemed to belong to the present in that place. The spirit of St. Francis and of St. Clare lives on."[1] We walked through slowly and took time to soak in the quiet atmosphere. After the bustle of the city streets and the enormity of the basilicas, this formed a good memory of Assisi to cap our journey. And it would have been good, except that the train station was next to the basilica of Santa Maria degli Angeli, and that, instead, became our final stop and memory of Assisi.

If San Damiano represents a beginning for Francis, then Santa Maria degli Angeli represents his end. It shelters the place he wanted to come to die.

The dome of Santa Maria degli Angeli dominates the valley

. . .

IN FRANCIS'S time the valley between Assisi and Perugia was different than it is now. Perugia—then an enemy of Assisi, a rival in the grand power struggles of the Middle Ages—would have been visible 20 kilometers to the west on a prominent hill. As the valley spreads below Assisi, one can see towns and villages, highways and train tracks, as well as vineyards and olive groves. But in Francis's time this was mostly forest, and it was in the middle of this forest that he and his followers eventually made their headquarters. A small chapel was loaned to them by the Benedictines of Mount Subasio. They named it Porziuncola, or the "Little Portion." It was here in 1226 that Francis came to die.

After Francis's death, pilgrims thronged the chapel. To protect it and to control the crowds, an enormous church was raised over it, and this is Santa Maria degli Angeli. Constructed between 1568 and 1684, it is one of the largest basilicas in the world and one of only two papal churches outside of Rome, the other one being the Basilica of San Francesco in Assisi.

With all my study and preparation about the sights of Assisi, this was one that I was not prepared for. The original chapel of Francis—three by five meters—was engulfed within the basilica. I stared at it in disbelief at first. It looked like a toy. I found the juxtaposition of the tiny chapel preserved inside the enormous basilica jarring, and I was not alone. A German pilgrim whom we met along the Way, Christine Schrati, described her visit to the Porziuncola similarly in her blog: "We also visited the Porziuncola... it remains in my memory as a completely unreal arrangement of two opposing buildings. The Porziuncola is a small chapel, formerly located in the forest below Assisi, the founding place of the Franciscan Order, a very simple stone house with a mystical charisma. Francesco died here. It is difficult to imagine the forest around it today, because in the 16th century a huge basilica, Santa Maria degli Angeli, was built over the chapel, which literally swallows it—and with it the humility, the *simplicity* and the unobstructed view to the future. For me, the surreal aspect of this arrangement ultimately remains."[2]

The Porziuncola, inside Santa Maria degli Angeli

I walked slowly through the Porziuncola and found its interior still quite modest and authentic. I paused a few moments to gaze around the inside of the basilica, and then I made my way out. This was my last visual impression of Assisi.[3]

HAD I spent longer inside the basilica, however, I would have noticed something else. Several yards away from that chapel was another small shrine that was an infirmary eight hundred years ago. This was the hut where Francis spent his last hours and where he died, and today it is called the Chapel of Transito. The basilica, in its magnificence, doesn't tell this story. But upon arriving home and researching more about the original Porziuncola, I read the account of his death—it moved me deeply, and I wish I had known it when I was there.

Francis had asked to come home to Assisi, specifically to the Porziuncola, to die. He spent his last days with his closest Franciscan brothers, especially some who had been with him from the very start. In his last hours, as his end approached, he asked them to strip him of his clothes and lay him naked on the earth as soon as he drew his last breath.

Il Poverello, the Little Poor Man, the one who loved the earth, the stones, the dirt, the birds, the flowers—in short, everything—this man wanted to come back into contact with that earth. The man who courted Lady Poverty, the one who was in love with God, who was eager to love everyone with whom he came into contact—this man wanted to return symbolically and literally to the earth. He loved the soil, and so he returned to it.

Lying there naked, he was once again—as he had been decades before up the hill in the courtyard of the bishop's palace, standing before the crowd—stripped of his clothes, completely free.

Afterword

I am writing this six months after returning from my last trek on the Way of St. Francis, and three and a half years since I first walked on it. As I reflected on my experiences and researched the writing of this book, three things stood out.

First, we need Francis and his faith more than ever. In an age of religious fundamentalism, we need his generous and gracious spirit. In a time of over-consumption that is despoiling and dangerously warming our planet—our only home—we need his reverence for the earth and his love for all humans and other creatures that inhabit it. His simple lifestyle points to the way out of our conspicuous over-consumption. His affection for and reconciliation to his hometown (and theirs to him) is an echo of hope into our fragmented and disconnected modern life. His non-violence is urgently needed in a world where there is too much warfare and far too much is spent on the military instead of for meeting basic human needs. My country—the United States—has more firearms than people, and mass-shootings are a daily occurrence.

Second, we need to walk more than ever. Walking bestows numerous health benefits—physical, mental, emotional, and spiritual. I live in a culture where many are unhealthy because of sedentary lifestyles. The average U.S. citizen walks less than two miles per day; our ancestors walked between eight and ten. Walking can help reduce weight, reduce cholesterol and lower blood pressure, increase bone density, boost moods, and improve brain health.[1] I find walking or hiking with others to be a healthy social practice, while walking alone helps to settle and clarify my thoughts. Being outside in nature is one of the simplest and cheapest things that any of us can do to improve our overall well-being. And if we walk to the store—it will even reduce our dependence on fossil fuels.

Lastly, we need *real* experiences more than ever. During the pandemic I heard repeatedly that "virtual" i.e., online experiences, were our future. Forget the office, forget the school, go online. I don't agree. We need *actual* experiences, with others—physical experiences. We need physical activity and social engagement with each other. Western society is addicted to screens, with the resultant negative conse-quences. Just this month a new twist on technology is all the rage—ChatGPT. I hear that it will make writing—and writers—obsolete. Someone asked me, humorously, why I didn't ask it to write this book for me. My answer is simple: I love to write and I hope to get better at it, even though I am well into my 60s. It is one of my favorite creative outlets. I will continue to write, to walk, and to write about walking as long as I can.

I close with these words from writer and farmer, Wendell Berry. "My wish is to live my life as fully as I can. In both our work and our leisure, I think, we should be so employed. And in our time this means that we must save ourselves from the products that we are asked to buy in order, ultimately, to replace ourselves."[2]

What a Franciscan sentiment.

Resources for pilgrims

Biographies of Saint Francis

For anyone interested in walking the Way of St. Francis, I recommend reading a biography before you go. There are numerous available in English. Two of my favorites are Don Spoto's *Reluctant Saint: The Life of Francis of Assisi* and Adrian's House's *Francis of Assisi: A Revolutionary Life.*

Guidebooks

Trekking the Way of St. Francis, by Sandy Brown is a must read for pilgrims, with lots of good historical and practical advice. Sandy pioneered much of the route from Florence to La Verna and then from Rieti to Rome. It is published by Cicerone Press, the foremost publisher of hiking books in the U.K.

The Way of St. Francis, by Matthew Harms has excellent maps, route advice, historical facts, all in a handy, pocketable size. Just published in 2023, it has the most up-to-date route and lodging information.

Navigation and information

Way markers, blazes and signs are getting better and better on the route, but I recommend that pilgrims download the GPX tracks for the entire route. GURU Maps and GAIA are top-notch apps with excellent offline maps that don't even require a cellular data plan to work.

Mobile phones and communication

I suggest that pilgrims get a local Sim card for their phones. Wifi is common at most lodging and many bars, but not always. TIM stores are ubiquitous in Tuscany, Umbria and Rome and TIM has the best coverage in the mountains. It's a good idea to get a mobile phone plan with data. I get a SIM card from TIM. 50G of data cost me 20 euros. Having an Italian phone number also helps with making phone reservations.

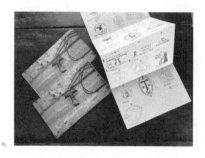

Pilgrim *credenziale*

Credenziali, or pilgrim passports are available from the Diocese of Gubbio and can be obtained online at https://

tinyurl.com/bdz784ee. I recommend three weeks delivery time. A credenziale is not required to obtain lodging, but you will need to present it in order to receive an testimonium from Assisi or Rome.

Finding Lodging on the Way of St. Francis

The Way of St Francis has many levels of accommodations for pilgrims, from hostels to hotels and everything in between, including rifugios, agriturismi, convents (often called Foresta or Foresteria) guest apartments and bed & breakfasts, just to name a few.

For people who have walked the Camino de Santiago with its hundreds of pilgrim-only albergues (hostels), where in the past it was easy and expected to simply show up and obtain a bed in a dormitory, there is a critical difference with the Way of St. Francis. First, and most importantly, along the Way of St. Francis, there are very few accommodations that are dedicated only for pilgrims and the often-limited space is available to anyone, whether they arrive by car or foot. On weekends or holidays lodging fills up quickly.

A second, and equally important difference, is that hosts expect to be contacted in advance, either by phone or email. One can, on occasion, simply "show up" but the host may not be available or lodging may be full. It is expected to make reservations ahead of time. The question is, how far ahead of time?

I think it comes down to assurance (security) versus flexibility. If you complete all of your lodging arrangements well in advance, then you are assured of a place to stay. But you sacrifice flexibility. When my wife and I first walked in 2019, we booked everything ahead for the two weeks; when we wanted to change our plans after the first day of walking, we were locked into our reservations for the entire time, which we regretted. It all worked out okay in the end (we bused to our next place) but we decided to do it differently in 2022 and only booked a day or two out, with a few exceptions:

- We always book our first night's lodging, even the first two. Depending on the time of year, we do that as soon as we can. Booking.com has a "cancellable reservation" filter and I always book something cancellable, just so I have a place. After that I may do more research and might change my mind, which I did this past year.

- We booked places that may be in high demand well ahead of time. For example, we were planning to be in La Verna on Easter, a very busy season, so I booked that about four months in advance. An email reservation and confirmation was sufficient.

Booking just a few days in advance meant we sometimes were out of luck. We did find more than once that a place was unavailable, but we found other, sometimes better options in the end, such as when we tried to book a place in Consuma but either found hosts out of town and their place unavailable, or accommodations full. But we were then offered the place in Villa, about seven kilometers ahead of Consuma, something we would not have considered. Elena, our host, even gave us a ride there, from Consuma. It turned out to be one of our favorite places and experiences. They gave us two meals and lots of good conversation. And then they recommended our next stay and then phoned ahead to make the reservation for us.

I do my research in advance, comparing lists of lodging. Several of those are online and the links are at the very end of this section. I also consulted three guidebooks. I prefer using places that are recommended in guidebooks or in the lists that are online, since they are supporting the pilgrimage route. Some of those places are also listed on booking.com, which makes the process very easy, since there is no issue with language. Otherwise, I try email, and if that's not available, then I phone. You may need to have some basic Italian for that! If you make direct contact by email or phone, that is often all you need to do; no need to give a credit card.

A few more things to keep in mind:

- Hosts can make you a lunch, but ask for that when you make your reservation. They can also call ahead to make reservations for you, saving time and issues with communication.

- Some places have a top-notch breakfast that will fill you up for hours. Some simply provide toast and coffee, and prepackaged items such as yogurt or sweets.

- Some places will hold a duffel or suitcase for you. This is helpful if you have to check walking poles, as I always do.

- Some places require cash; some take credit card; some give a discount if you pay in cash. Often there is an extra head tax required by the locality of one or two euros, which you need to pay in cash.

- In small towns, fewer people speak English. In larger towns you may find more English speakers. Younger people often speak some English. Italy also has many immigrants from all over the world and I found that more of them spoke excellent English than I would have expected!

- A room in Italian is *camera*, a very confusing cognate for English speakers.

- A *convent* in Italy is a monastery, either for men or women.

I have lists of lodging on my website. Go to russeanes.com or visit https://tinyurl.com/2p97cd4p

Groups and tours

The Way of St. Francis lends itself well to groups. Pilgrim Paths (https://pilgrimpaths.com) offers guided tours for groups of up to 12 people.

Touch the stones

Notes

Introduction: Francis and His Ways

1. It can easily be confused with some other historical routes, such as the *Via Francigena*, which starts in Canterbury, England, and crosses the English Channel on its way through France and Switzerland before winding its way across Italy to Rome. That route is over 2,000 kilometers long and takes about three months to walk. Another, the *Camino Frances*, or "French Route," is the most commonly walked section of the Camino de Santiago, from St. Jean Pied-de-Port in France, to Santiago de Compostela.

2. *The Way of St. Francis* was written by Sandy Brown and first published in 2015 by Cicerone. It was the first guidebook for the complete Florence-to-Rome route and divides the walk into 28 stages. *On the Road with Saint Francis* was written and published in Italian in 2004 by Angela Maria Seracchioli and details a route from La Verna to Rieti. Terre di Mezzo published that Italian edition and then in 2013 an excellent English translation. Most recently, in 2023 Matthew Harms wrote *The Way of St. Francis*, part of the series of Pilgrimage Guides published by Village to Village Press, which divides the route into 27 stages. For more details on each, see the Bibliography.

3. For Americans, that's over 52,000 feet, which is 10 miles. Climbing.

4. Rohr, Richard, "A Prime Attractor," daily meditations, May 17, 2015, https://cac.org/daily-meditations/a-prime-attractor-2017-06-05.

5. Rohr, Richard, "A Prime Attractor," daily meditations.

6. House, Adrian, *Francis of Assisi: A Revolutionary Life*, p.11.

7. At the time Francis visited the Sultan, his preaching would have been considered proselytizing and therefore punishable by death. This makes the Sultan's respect all the more incredible.

8. *Gospel of Luke*, 9:23.

1. An Arduous Journey

1. The curious reader might be happy to know that we returned to Florence the day after we reached Assisi and spent three days there as "ordinary" tourists.

2. Constructed in the late 13th and early 14th centuries at the northern boundary of Florence, San Gallo—site of a convent ironically named after an Irish monk of the late 6th and early 7th centuries—was the main northern gate in the city walls, on the principal route to Bologna. Two similar gates still exist in the city, but the old walls are mostly gone, cleared out in the 19th century as the city expanded. The outline of the old city walls can still be traced by the Viali di Circonvallazione, or "ring road" on modern maps of Florence, a pattern similar to what is found in many old European cities. The walls were demolished in the mid-19th century and replaced with a series of wide boulevards, inspired by what had been done in Paris.

3. GPX tracks are routes recorded by previous walkers with GPS (Global Positioning System) that can be followed on a mobile phone app, such as GURU or GAIA, both of which I use. They are especially helpful when route markers are sparse.

2. Into the Mountains

1. *Pontis* is Latin for bridge, so Pontassieve is "bridge over the Sieve."
2. Saint Anthony is the patron of lost things.
3. The *tabacchi*, short for *tabaccheria*, is the one-stop convenience shop in Italian towns for cigarettes, bus tickets, postage stamps, souvenirs, and such. It is usually indicated by a large blue or black "T."
4. In an Italian bar or café, you only settle up your bill as you are leaving.
5. *Buon Cammino* is the greeting in Italian from one pilgrim to another, something like, "have a good trip."
6. On the European hiking trails, distances are given in time as well as kilometers.

3. Over the Pass

1. During 2022, Elena and Luca had more than 500 pilgrims stay in their B&B and 80 in their rifugio. Luca is also the president of the *Via Francesco Tuscana*, the Association of the Way of St. Francis, in Tuscany.
2. When booking lodging, I suggest asking your current host if can phone ahead for you.
3. It was particularly important to me, when I walked the Camino de Santiago four years earlier, that I walk the whole way. I needed to prove something to myself, and I proved it. I no longer need to do that. This is a lesson that comes with age and, I hope, wisdom.

4. Into the Forest

1. In Italy, a *foresteria* is a guesthouse or hostel inside a convent. Convents in Italy are not gender specific and are dwellings for men as well as women.
2. At its most basic, a *rifugio* is a rustic mountain hut with no running water or heat. We passed a few of those along the way. The term can also refer to a modern hostel with dorm-style beds and even private rooms and meals.
3. The name is derived from *Campus Maldoli*, which means "field of Maldolo."
4. The Via Romea Germanica is an historic route, 2,200 kilometers, starting in Germany and crossing through Austria and the Tyrolean Alps into Italy and ending in Rome. Its history dates back to the 13th century.

5. Brother Wind, Sister Water

1. The translation above, from the Umbrian dialect of Italian, is from https://cafod.org.uk/pray/prayer-resources/canticle-of-the-sun.
2. Poggio is a common place name in Italy, and there are dozens along the Way of St. Francis. It is translated as "hill" or "mount."

6. That Rock 'Twixt Tiber and the Arno

1. *Sasso spicco* is translated various ways into English, something like "promontory" or "rock face," it describes more than one of Francis's hermitages.
2. Francis may not have been the first person to exhibit the stigmata. According to Elizabeth T. Knuth, "Mary of Oignies may have been the first stigmatist, having received the stigmata twelve years prior to Francis of Assisi's famous experience." The source of this is a paper Knute wrote in December 1992, which was originally online, source now unavailable.
3. Saint Bonaventure, a contemporary of Francis, was commissioned to write Francis's first biography in 1228, at the same time that Francis was canonized. But the most popular book about Francis's life and miracles is *The Little Flowers of Saint Francis*, published a century after his death. In my opinion, the book is so laden with miracles that it becomes almost impossible to see the real man behind them.

7. Pilgrimage as Ritual

1. Floods later that spring actually closed some parts of this route, from Città di Castello to Gubbio, showing the occasional hazards that exist in some of the mountainous sections.
2. See Martin Palmer and Nigel Palmer, *Sacred Britain: A Guide to the Sacred Sites and Pilgrim Routes of England, Scotland and Wales*, pp. 22–24.
3. Derry Brabbs, *Pilgrimage: The Great Pilgrimage Routes of Britain and Europe*, p. 6.
4. Robert Macfarlane, "Rites of Way: Behind the Pilgrimage Revival," *The Guardian*, June 5, 2012 [page number?]. See also his book, *The Old Ways: A Journey on Foot*.
5. In the Exodus story, the Israelites were provided each day at dawn with manna, a foodlike substance. It had to be used that day and could not be hoarded since it would spoil. See Exodus, Chapter 16.

8. Stones and Wolves

1. *Little Flowers of St. Francis, pp. 34-5*
2. Vauchez, André, *Francis of Assisi: The Life and Afterlife of a Medieval Saint*, p. 276.

9. The Ambience of History

1. James Herriot, *The Best of James Herriot*, p. 17.
2. Sarel Eimerl, *The World of Giotto*, p. 55.

10. The Opposite Direction

1. Peter was the first Bishop of Rome, and the Basilica houses his remains. He was probably martyred on this spot in the first century C.E.
2. In 2013, Jorge Mario Bergoglio became the first Pope from Latin America and the first one to take the name Francis. The name is intentional, indicating a deemphasis on the power and wealth of the Roman Catholic Church.

11. Unexpected Paths

1. Broccolini is technically in the broccoli family and consists of tender

shoots of broccoli with small florets. It originated in Asia. I'm not sure if that's what I had here; it tasted and looked just like boiled spinach.

12. The Work of Walking

1. This road dates back to the first century B.C.E., when the Sabines used this path to access the salt "pans" at Ostia, east of the city of Rome. Later the Romans used it to access new salt beds on the Adriatic Sea. Salt was a valuable commodity in ancient times, and Roman soldiers were paid, in part, in salt. From the word *salt* we derive the word *salary*, which was cut if a soldier was "not worth his salt."
2. I learned from Ed that a Roman mile was 1,000 double-paces (*mille* in Latin, the origin of the American English word *mile*).

13. Good Morning, Good People

1. You can still visit Marmore Falls. A hydro dam holds back the water, and it is released twice per day to feed electric turbines. The entrance to the park lies along the Way of St. Francis.
2. San Felice all'Acqua is Saint Felix, or "Felice" in Italian, who produced a miraculous spring out of a rock in the ground, to satisfy the thirst of field workers on an unbearably hot day. Besides this rural church, at the site of the miraculous spring, the 18th century parish church in Cantalice is called by the same name and holds San Felice's remains.
3. There is actually a hermitage and sanctuary of Francis' here at this convent as well.
4. Thomas of Celano, *The First Life of Francis,* quoted in *Francis of Assisi, A Revolutionary Life*, p. 85.

14. Poetry in Action

1. Linda B. Francke, *On the Road with Francis of Assisi,* p. 189.
2. Some art historians credit Francis with making religious art more "earthy" and realistic, rather than remote and otherworldly.
3. In Italy, I always found heavily trafficked roads to be more dangerous than any rocky or steep mountain pass.
4. Maximo Fusarelli, *Sanctuaries of the Rieti Valley,* p. 28. Farfa, several miles south, was one of the largest and most influential Benedictine convents in the region.
5. Any religious order under the Roman Catholic Church needs to have an approved "Rule," which is a form of life and discipline approved by

the Pope. Francis never intended to formulate a new religious order, but in order to be accepted by the institutional church, created a rule in 1222 (subsequently lost) and replaced it with the one written in 1223 at Fonte Colombo.

6. Adrian House, *Francis of Assisi: A Revolutionary Life*, p. 9
7. David Steindl-Rast, "Recollections of Merton's Last Days in the West." https://grateful.org/resource/recollections-of-thomas-mertons-last-days-in-the-west. Also referenced in *A Hidden Wholeness: The Visual World of Thomas Merton*, by John Howard Griffin and Thomas Merton, p. 49.

15. The Green Heart of Italy

1. All of the guidebook descriptions are in the north-to-south direction, from Florence to Rome. GPS navigation using GPX files is explained in Chapter 2, with links to find them in the Resources section at the end of this book.
2. The name comes from Giosuè Carducci (1835–1907), the Italian poet laureate.
3. Some variants do lead up into the mountains, but we didn't take those.

16. Mystical Assisi

1. Richard Rohr, *Eager to Love*, p. xv.
2. In 2019, when Jane and I made our first pilgrimage to Assisi, we were told that about 18,000 people arrive per year and ask to receive a *testimonium*. Contrast that with over 400,000 who arrive per year in Santiago and receive the *Compostela* or certificate of completion.
3. It is known as "Hill of Hell" because it was used for executions.
4. Donald Spoto, *Reluctant Saint: The Life of Francis of Assisi, pp. 211-12*
5. Francis's family home is a tourist landmark in Assisi, and in it you can see the storeroom where Francis was supposedly imprisoned. It stands just above the Chiesa Maggiore Maria, but it is not certain that this was actually his family's home.
6. Richard Rohr, *Eager to Love: The Alternative Way of Francis of Assisi*, p. 39.
7. See the Gospel of Matthew 6:25-34. Francis modeled his life after passages like this, which stress trust in God rather than money.
8. Donald Spotto, *Reluctant Saint: The Life of Francis of Assisi*, p. 57. I personally wonder if Francis' refusal to allow his friars to accept money for payment was rooted his own family's history with money as an end in itself, partly exhibited by his father's demand that the bishop give him back the sack of coins.

17. Farewell to Francis

1. R. P. Nicola Giandomenico, *Art and History: Assisi,* p. 113.
2. Translated from Christine Schrati, "Pace e Bene – Cammino #18," http://www.schrati.net.
3. I mused much later that Santa Maria degli Angeli was a parallel to the bishop's robe that had been draped over Francis when he broke with his family. The robe had symbolized both the need to hide his nakedness and to declare the protection of the church.

Afterword

1. *New England Journal of Medicine Study,* 2001
2. Wendell Berry, *What Are People For?* p.190

Bibliography

Armitage, Simon, *Walking Home: A Poet's Journey*. New York: Liveright Publishing Corporation, 2013.

Berry, Wendell, *What Are People For?* New York: North Point Press, 1990.

Boers, Arthur, *Living into Focus: Choosing What Matters in an Age of Distraction*. Grand Rapids: Brazos, 2012.

Brabbs, Derry, *Pilgrimage: The Great Pilgrimage Routes of Britain and Europe*. London: Quarto Publishing plc, 2017.

Brown, Sandy, *Trekking the Way of St. Francis: From Florence to Assisi and Rome*. Milnthorpe, Cicerone: 2015.

Chittister, Joan, *The Gift of Years: Growing Older Gracefully*. New York: Blue-Bridge, 2008.

Cousineau, Phil, *The Art of Pilgrimage: The Seeker's Guide to Making Travel Sacred*. Coral Gables: Conari Press, 2021.

Deloris, Vine Jr., *God is Red*. Golden: Fulcrum Publishing 2003

Eimerl, Sarel, *The World of Giotto*. Morristown: Time, Inc., 1967.

Francke, Linda Bird, *On the Road with Francis of Assisi: A Timeless Journey Through Umbria and Tuscany, and Beyond*. New York: Random House, 2005.

Fusarelli, Brother Massimo, *The Franciscan Sanctuaries of the Rieti Valley*. Genova: B. N. Marconi, 1999.

Giandomenico, Nicola, *Art and History: Assisi*. Florence: World Publisher.

Hari, Johann, *Stolen Focus: Why You Can't Pay Attention and How to Think Deeply Again*. New York: Crown, 2022.

Griffin, John Howard and Merton, Thomas, *A Hidden Wholeness: The Visual World of Thomas Merton*. Boston: Houghton Mifflin, 1970.

Harms, Matthew, *The Way of St. Francis (Village to Village Guides)*. Harrisonburg: Village to Village Press, 2023.

Herriot, James, *The Best of James Herriot: Favourite Memories of a Country Vet*. New York: St. Martin's Press, 1982.

Hopkins, Gerard Manley, *The Poems of Gerard Manley Hopkins*. London: Oxford U.P., 1967.

House, Adrian, *Francis of Assisi: A Revolutionary Life*. Mahwah: Hidden Springs, 2001.

Macfarlane, Robert, "Rites of Way: Behind the Pilgrimage Revival," *The

Guardian, June 15, 2012. https://www.theguardian.com/books/2012/jun/15/rites-of-way-pilgrimage-walks

Macfarlane, Robert, *The Old Ways: A Journey on Foot.* New York: Penguin Books, 2012.

Moffat, Alistair, *The Hidden Ways: Scotland's Forgotten Roads.* Edinburgh: Canongate, 2017.

Moffat, Alistair, *Tuscany, A History.* Edinburgh: Birlinn Limited, 2011.

Nooteboom, Gees, *Roads to Santiago: A Modern-Day Pilgrimage Through Spain.* Orlando: Harcourt, 1992. Translated by Ina Rilke.

Okey, Thomas (translator), *The Little Flowers of Saint Francis.* New York: Dover Publications, 2003. (author unknown)

O'Mara, Shane, *In Praise of Walking.* New York: Random House, 2019.

Palmer, Martin and Palmer, Nigel, *Sacred Britain: A Guide to the Sacred Sites and Pilgrim Routes of England, Scotland and Wales,* London: Judy Piatkus (Publishers) LTD, 1997.

Pilgrim, Peace, *Peace Pilgrim: Her Life and Work.* Santa Fe: Ocean Tree Books, 2013.

Rohr, Richard, *Falling Upward: A Spirituality for the Two Halves of Life.* San Francisco: Jossey Bass, 2011.

Rohr, Richard, *Eager to Love:* The Alternative Way of Francis of Assisi. Cincinnati: Franciscan Media, 2014.

Seracchioli, Angela Maria, *On the Road with Saint Francis.* Milan: Terre de mezzo, 2004. Translated by Leaslie Ray.

Silvestri, Adriana, *Magic Moments in Florence.* Florence: La Mandragora, 1999.

Spoto, Donald, *Reluctant Saint: The Life of Francis of Assisi.* New York: Penguin Compass, 2002.

Thomson, Ian, *Dante's Divine Comedy: A Journey Without End.* London: House of Zeus Ltd, 2018.

Vauchez, Andre, *Francis of Assisi: The Life and Afterlife of a Medieval Saint.* New Haven: Yale University Press, 2012. Translated by Michael F. Cusato

Acknowledgments

I am indebted to the many people who helped make this book a reality. It times it felt like a marathon, with a very long sprint to the end.

First, I thank my wife Jane, who encouraged this project from the start and who was my willing and eager walking companion for most of this journey. She is my first reader, strongest critic, and careful editor. I am fortunate and grateful that she has embraced my passion for trekking.

I thank my two editors, Susan Lahey and Heath Lynn Silberfeld, who helped with syntax, grammar, spelling, punctuation, but most of all helped shape this into a coherent whole. Editors always make me a better writer, and I have a long way to go.

I thank my two sons, Andre and Nathan, who designed and helped with the cover for the book.

All of us who walk this route are indebted to Sandy Brown, who pioneered the Way of St. Francis with his first guidebook from Cicerone Press and has helped create and popularize this route for English speakers. Sandy also provided lists of lodging, GPX files and created a great Facebook group which is supportive and helpful to all.

I also want to thank Mattew Harms and David Landis who kindly lent me an early draft of their new guidebook *The Way of St. Francis,* from Village to Village Press. Besides being a helpful guide for the journey, I was happy to provide corrections to the text for them as well as photographs for their excellent and handy resource for pilgrims. David was also one of the first who encouraged me to write a book about what it's like to walk the Way of St. Francis.

I want to thank Ed Vaesson for joining me spontaneously for four days of walking, and for putting up my with my snoring. Ed also kindly allowed the use of material from his blog, which helped give me another perspective on the journey. I hope to see you again on the trail!

I also thank Christine Schrati, whom we met along the way from Florence, who shared her insights on the Way of St. Francis and allowed me to use some of her writings and observations.

I thank Luca and Elena Piantini for offering excellent hospitality at Rifugio San Jacopo and also for sending me historical material about the Way of St. Francis in Tuscany.

Lastly, I thank the baristas at Black Sheep Coffee, here in Harrisonburg, where I wrote most of this book. They always anticipated what I wanted: 12 oz. coffee, in a large cup, with a saucer.

Also by Russ Eanes

The Walk of a Lifetime: 500 Miles on the Camino de Santiago

What Readers Said about the Walk of a Lifetime

Books on the pilgrimage to Santiago de Compostela are many, but few capture the richness of the experience as well as Russ Eanes' *The Walk of a Lifetime*. It merits a slow reading so that it's spiritual and human truths might be deeply savored. Russ shares not just details of his walk along the Camino de Santiago in Spain, but the grace that carried him forward and left its mark on his heart forever. I am grateful for the telling of his pilgrim story for it is the story of many.

—Kevin Codd, author of *To the Field of Stars: A Pilgrim's Journey to Santiago de Compostela*.

Reading his book was like getting to walk the Camino all over again. As I plan my own return to the Camino this year, reading Eanes' account of the villages and their lessons gave me butterflies as I begin to anticipate my own journey… Some Camino memoirs make you wish that you had had the opportunity to walk alongside the author. Eanes' is one of those. And yet he does invite us to walk alongside him on his journey, sharing with us the scenery as well as his innermost thoughts and struggles. Walking with him was an absolute delight.

–Roni Jackson-Kerr, reviewed in March 2020 *La Concha*, quarterly newsletter of the American Pilgrims on the Camino

Reading Russ Eanes' *The Walk of a Lifetime* was the next best thing to doing the entire Camino. I felt like I was walking with him every step of the way. If you can, do the Camino. If you can't (at least this year), read the book.

—David Brubaker, Dean Eastern Mennonite University

About the Author

Russ Eanes is a writer, walker and cyclist from Harrisonburg, Virginia, where he lives with his wife Jane, three of his adult children and five of his seven grandchildren. He also enjoys traveling, gardening, reading and photography. In 2018 he "downshifted" to experience a less hectic pace of life and is now putting to use several decades' experience in the publishing business to work as an editor, publishing coach and consultant. He also leads walking and hiking tours, including tours on the Way of St. Francis.

This is second book.

For photos and more information about his books or tours, to go RussEanes.com